A
Practical
Guide
to
Training
Hawks
and
Falcons

A FALCONRY MANUAL

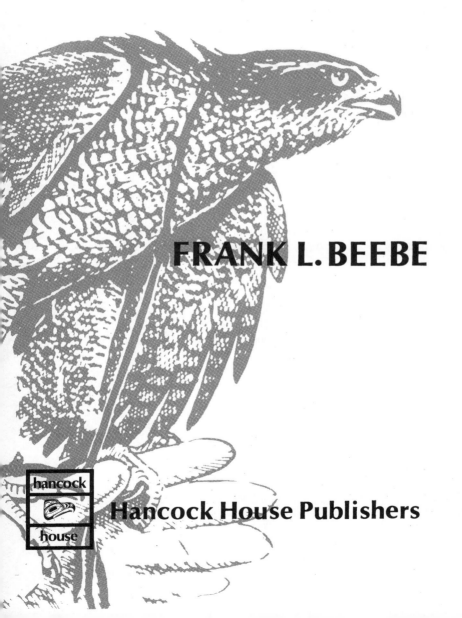

FRANK L. BEEBE

Hancock House Publishers

ISBN-10: 0-88839-978-2
ISBN-13: 978-0-88839-978-6
Copyright © 1984 Frank Beebe

Fourth printing 2008

Cataloging in Publication Data

Beebe, Frank L. (Frank Lyman). 1914 –
    A falconry manual

    Includes index.
    Bibliography: p.
    ISBN 0-88839-978-2

First ed. published as: Hawks, falcons & falconry.
Saanichton, B.C.: Hancock House, 1976.

    1. Falcons. 2. Hawks. 3. Falconry. I. Title.
SK321.B37 1983   799.2'32   C83-091325-4

Printed in Indonesia — TK PRINTING

We acknowledge the financial support of the Government of Canada through the Book Publishing Industry Development Program (BPIDP) for our publishing activities.

Published simultaneously in Canada and the United States by

HANCOCK HOUSE PUBLISHERS LTD.
19313 Zero Avenue, Surrey, B.C. Canada V3S 9R9
(604) 538-1114 Fax (604) 538-2262

HANCOCK HOUSE PUBLISHERS
1431 Harrison Avenue, Blaine, WA U.S.A. 98230-5005
(604) 538-1114 Fax (604) 538-2262

Website: **www.hancockhouse.com**
Email: **sales@hancockhouse.com**

Table of Contents

Introduction 7
Birds of Falconry 9

Falcons 13
Kestrel 17
Merlin 21
Aplomado 25
Prairie 27
Peregrine 33
Gyrfalcons and Sakers 41

Hawks 47
Sharp-shinned 49
Goshawk 55
Cooper's 63
Red-tailed 67
Ferruginous 73
Harris 79

Game, Vermin, Predators and Wildlife 83
Falconry Equipment 95
Capturing Wild Raptors 111
Eyess versus Passager 123
Care and Attention 129
Training 137
Accipiters 144
Falcons 150

Suggested Readings 193
Index 196

Cover photograph: Saker falcon by Abdul Rahman Al Saoud

Gyrfalcon — Adult Female. F.L. BEEBE

Introduction

This book is presented as a summary of practical information on the training of your hawk or falcon. It draws on my earlier works in this field: *North American Falconry and Hunting Hawks*, 1960; *Hawks, Falcons and Falconry*, 1976; and finally my major work covering the history, training and behavior of birds of prey, *The Compleat Falconer*, 1992 (Hancock House Publishers).

The Eurasion history of falconry reaches as far back in time as the recorded history of mankind. However, in North America everything pertaining to falconry has occurred in a time-span of only sixty years. The first falcons in North America of which there is any record were trained and flown in the eastern United States shortly after World War I. However, until the publication of *North American Falconry and Hunting Hawks*, there was no comprehensive source of information available which dealt with the techniques of either capturing or training hawks and falcons.

Until some kind of administrative common-sense was made of the foregoing, especially in the United States, the writing of a popular book on falconry could not be properly undertaken. This problem arose because prior to 1983 in the United States the fundamental question, "where can I obtain a hawk or falcon?," could not be clearly answered. Now, for the first time since the continent-wide protection of North America raptorial birds in the late 1960s, there is a clear answer. This answer is the right of purchase. The novice can obtain a domestic-bred hawk or falcon from a raptor breeder the same way he can obtain a horse, dog, cockatiel or canary. Ownership is transferred with the payment of the purchase price.

Publisher's Note:

It is also rewarding that with the re-establishment of the peregrine falcon back into much of its former range, the result of captive breeding and hacking techniques pioneered by falconers, and the consequent downgrading of the bird's endangered status and the recovery of many birds of prey populations (in all likelihood this will continue to an over abundance and a movement to eventually villainize the predator again) that many jurisdictions of North America again permit the capturing of wild hawks and falcons. This adds the option of providing both fresh blood lines for captive breeders and the excitement of capturing your own bird. Falconry is an ancient sport with contemporary objectives of yielding a maximum recreational return for little or no drain on the wild populations.

David Hancock
Publisher, and former falconer

Birds of Falconry

Hawks and Falcons

The training of a hawk or a falcon is not a difficult task. It equates rather well to the training of a field dog, such as a pointer or a retriever, and is rather less difficult, and far less dangerous, than training a horse. Certainly no beginner needs to know the scientific name, geographical origin, nesting, reproductive behavior and natural prey species of a particular kind of hawk or falcon before he can successfully train and hunt with such a bird. To avoid disappointment, every novice should know the fundamental differences between hawks and falcons before attempting to acquire a bird. It is also a real advantage to know enough about the different kinds of hawks and falcons to avoid confusion over superficial similarities in species and age-class.

Anyone without knowledge of hawks and falcons who attends a falconry meet for the first time is certain to be confused about the birds he sees and what he is told about them. It seems the comparatively small size of most falconry birds surprises the novice. Contemporary television coverage, usually done with telephoto lenses and presented in slow-motion, leads people to think of them as being much larger than they really are. When an expert first tells a novice a little blue-gray bird no larger than a crow is actually a fine adult male of the glamorized peregrine falcon, the initial reaction is nearly always one of disappointment and incredulity. Surely the glamorous peregrine, the falcon of falcons, is larger and more impressive than that little thing? Some are, but some are also considerably smaller. Nearby sits another blue-gray bird, a little larger perhaps, but almost exactly the same color. An expert will tell the novice this bird is neither a peregrine nor even a falcon. This bird is an adult tiercel (male) American goshawk. Close at hand is another bird which looks different: over two feet tall, pale, reddish-tawny, streaked with dark brown, wings and tail cross-barred dark brown, a pale-yellow eye glaring from below a white eyebrow and huge, heavy-clawed feet. This bird is also a goshawk.

How can this be? If the blue-gray goshawk looks so much like the blue-gray peregrine, how is it possible the big red-brown bird is also a goshawk? The answer is the red-brown bird is a first-year female European goshawk. For the novice, this answer is not satisfactory at all, even though it may serve as a good lesson in learning to identify raptors. The first thing one must learn is there is a greater difference in size between females and males and in color between first-year birds and adults of the same species than there is between different species. When the obviously different are really the same and the apparently very much alike are entirely different, something requires sorting out. The two people looking at the same three birds are certainly not seeing them in the same way. The novice must learn to discern just what it is which makes the different appear the same and the same appear different.

Students of avian anatomy say hawks and falcons, however much alike some of them may appear, originate from different ancestral lines. Falcons worldwide, regardless of size or color, have certain distinct characteristics which mark them as falcons. Falconers have known and recognized these characteristics for thousands of years.

Look now at the six silhouettes. The first three are profiles of sitting raptors. Because the birds of the three species named are all about the same size, the one at the left has been labelled "gyrfalcon," the one in the middle "goshawk" and the one at the right "red-tailed hawk." The first two are nearly identical except for slightly smaller

Gyrfalcon

Goshawk

head and slightly shorter wingtips of the center silhouette. However-er, note the silhouette at the left and the one at the right, labelled "gyrfalcon" and "red-tailed hawk," are exactly the same. The next three silhouettes look entirely different, but they have the same name labels in the same sequence. These silhouettes are of the same three kinds of birds as viewed from directly in front or behind with spread wings. From this viewpoint, the falcon and goshawk, though significantly different, are nevertheless more alike than are the falcon and the red-tail. Strong similarities in color and feather-patterns between adult goshawks and adult-plumaged gray-phase gyrfalcons are sometimes so close as to make them impossible to distinguish from one another, even in good light when they are seen perched at some distance. The silhouettes show how the birds immediately identify themselves the moment they take wing.

Falconers refer to falcons as longwings and hawks as shortwings because of the pronounced and constant difference in the flight outline of falcons from all other raptors. When seen close at hand,

Red-tailed hawk

there are other constant characteristics which also mark all falcons. The eyes are always dark brown, the beak has a sharp downward projection or "tooth" just behind the hooked tip, the feet have small circular scales rather than transverse scutes and the claws on the three forward toes are about equal in size.

The flight silhouette of forest hawks — birds known to falconers as shortwings and to science as accipiters — are, as shown, quite different. Except for the training of certain eagles, traditional Eurasian falconry was entirely confined to the training of falcons and forest hawks. In North America, a second group of savannah-grassland hawks, known to science as buteos, has come into widespread use. Some of these hawks are as willing as any goshawk to pursue ground quarries — particularly rabbits or hares — in terrain covered with trees and brush or across open lands. Buteos are neither as swift nor as agile as forest hawks, but they are easier to train and they are much less temperamental and unpredictable in the field. One of these, the Harris's hawk, a bird completely unknown to falconry in 1960, is now the species most widely used in North America.

Forest hawks differ from falcons in their flight appearance. They differ less so when perched, although the longer tail and shorter wingtips are then distinctive. These hawks often have pale eyes, especially during the first year. However, hawks resemble falcons rather closely in color and in markings as well as in the profound changes in color and in markings which occur in both genera at the time of the first moult. Except when they are seen perched in silhouette — when certain buteos and large falcons may be quite indistinguishable — the buteos are different in flight and color from both falcons and forest hawks.

The falcons evolved as fast-flying, bird-hunting predators of open landscapes — tundras, grasslands, deserts, moorlands and sea-coasts. They also occur and breed in savannah grasslands and forests, but in such regions they hunt across the open areas or above the forest canopy. Conversely, hawks evolved as in-forest hunters of birds, small mammals and reptiles. Most species available to falconers will pursue either birds or mammals in timbered or brushy areas as well as across open land.

Any hawk or falcon can be entirely trained for flights on artificial quarry (lures), but if the purpose of acquiring a raptor for training is to eventually hunt real quarries, the novice should try to acquire the kind of hawk or falcon best suited to the landscape over which the bird is to hunt and to the kind of quarry which most commonly occurs on that land. One does not acquire a peregrine for hunting tree squirrels nor a Harris's hawk for hunting sharp-tailed grouse or ptarmigan. Some areas have suitable terrain and quarries for either a hawk or a falcon or both, but no novice should attempt to train both types of hunting bird at the same time.

Generally speaking, falcons are easier for most novices to understand, handle and train than any of the forest hawks. Two buteoine hawks, the red-tailed hawk and the Harris's hawk, are also good beginner's birds, especially the latter. Harris's hawks are so easy to train, become so attached to their trainer once trained, are so adaptable to a wide range of quarries and terrain and are so willing to reproduce in captivity that they have become the most popular of all hawks of North American falconry in less than two decades. To a remarkable degree, female Harris's hawks have displaced both goshawks and red-tailed hawks for hunting rabbits and hares while tiercels are nearly the equal of goshawks for hunting pond and ditch ducks and of Cooper hawks for hunting quail and western cottontail rabbits. As a result, Harris's hawks are best for the novice. Furthermore, they are the most easily acquired and most inexpensive of all North American raptors. (Note: Only red-tailed hawks and American kestrels are permitted for apprentice falconers in the U.S.)

Falcons

In 1964, when *North American Falconry and Hunting Hawks* was first published, it was reasonably easy to accurately describe the six kinds of native falcons then available to anyone in North America. At that time, no falcon of any kind had been domestically bred on this continent and only one successful attempt at breeding falcons had been made anywhere in the world. All six of the distinctly different and easily described species were officially listed as vermin and were available for capture with no permits of any kind required. These species, listed from largest to smallest were gyrfalcons, peregrine falcons, prairie falcons, aplomado falcons, merlins and kestrels. Equally describable were the three fairly distinct subspecies of peregrine falcons known as Anatum (continental) peregrines, Tundrius (arctic) peregrines and Pealei (Peale's) peregrines, the big falcons of the northwest coast. A scant two decades later, it is impossible to describe many of the falcons falcon breeders produce and equally impossible to describe, or even to give a name to, the new breed of eastern mid-continental peregrine. This situation, rising from the continent-wide protection of falcons in the mid-1960s and the restrictions imposed later on their capture and use, is so unexpected and so improbable as to require explanation.

In 1964, I predicted the imminent domestication of falcons, especially peregrines, and was for a time personally involved some of the pioneer work toward that end. The idea took root and proceeded so quickly that by 1970 there were at least sixty known private raptor breeding projects on the continent. However, the same year also saw peregrines in the United States officially declared an extinct species east of the Mississippi River and officially declared an endangered species continent-wide; gyrfalcons were also officially declared an endangered species and all other falcons were listed as "threatened." These listings instantly prohibited the sale or the purchase of any falcon native to North America and also any import or export, except by way of scientific permits issued to government agencies or scientific institutions. I personally maintained at the time, and still do, that all of this maneuvering was done far less for the reason of saving peregrine falcons from imminent extinction than it was to contain the growth of falconry through institutionalizing the breeding of falcons. In any case, the private breeders had about eight years of lead-time which was to prove decisive. The legal situation, which abruptly debarred private breeders from selling their birds, remained apparently unchanged from 1970 to 1983. However, things began to erode in unforseeable ways.

By the early 1970s, it was already known that not only are most falcons willing to reproduce in natural pairs through natural incubation, but also the use of the methods of contemporary poultry breeders — artificial insemination and incubation of eggs — could easily more than double the natural rate of reproduction. With these techniques at hand and private competition contained by law, the institutionalized, public-funded breeding projects at Cornell University in the United States and at Wainwright, Alberta, Canada, began production of falcons, mostly peregrine falcons. These high-profile, publicized programs were oriented to "the reestablishment of this esteemed species in those areas from which it had disappeared." From the onset, there appears to have been a major policy difference between the two projects, particularly in the precieved need to produce birds quickly for publicized release. Of the two, the Canadian project appears now to have been either the more responsible or the least beset with competition. If the reports the Canadian project published are accurate, no peregrines other than those bred from the original mid-continental anatum subspecies have been released to the wild populations. At Cornell, a different approach was taken. With peregrines officially declared an extinct species east of the Mississippi River, no serious attempt was made to obtain native, mid-continental peregrines for breeding stock. Instead, adults from diverse sources were procured as quickly as possible and the peregrines released as part of the American "reestablishment" program were a mix of Spanish, northern European and all three North American subspecies.

Certainly, the American program has been more populist than scientific. I doubt very much if peregrines were indeed completely

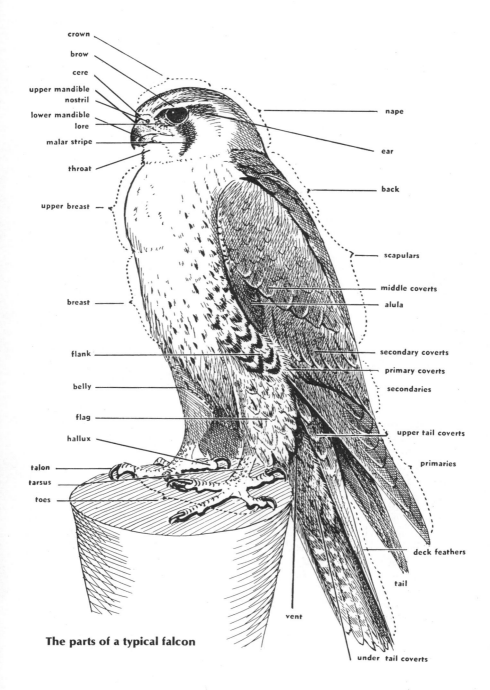

crown
brow
cere
upper mandible
nostril
lower mandible
lore
malar stripe
throat
upper breast
breast
flank
belly
flag
hallux
talon
tarsus
toes

nape
ear
back
scapulars
middle coverts
alula
secondary coverts
primary coverts
secondaries
upper tail coverts
primaries
deck feathers
tail
vent
under tail coverts

The parts of a typical falcon

extinct east of the Mississippi when they were officially declared extinct. From 1980 onwards, no peregrine falcons breeding anywhere in the eastern mid-latitudes of North America will be scientifically describeable because the large-scale American release of mongrel falcons completely negates the Canadian pure-stock re-introductions in southern Ontario and Quebec. To North American falconry, these deliberate releases of peregrines of mixed ancestry have done more good than harm. The accidental escape of a North American falconer's peregrine of equally-mixed ancestry or even from a different part of the world can be no cause for complaint.

The scientifically-questionable aspects of at least the American institutional falcon "re-establishment" program eroded its claim to any exclusive right to breed falcons. Meanwhile, private breeders, prohibited from the purchase or sale of any falcon describeable as being any of the native North American species, soon found they could produce, sell and, in Canada, export falcons which could not be described as being any one of them. It turns out falcons of all kinds are so closely related genetically as to be mutually fertile. Through artificial insemination and incubator hatching, virtually any species cross seems now to be possible. Further, some of these hybrid falcons are known to be still fertile and three-species crosses have already been produced.

Hybrids have the unique characteristic of being more clearly defined by what they are not than by what they are. Thus, a hybrid gyrfalcon peregrine can not be identified as being either of these nor any other known species. Therefore, its sale cannot be prohibited nor its ownership disputed. This type of bird can be a beautiful, distinctive and highly effective bird for falconry combining the best of both parent stocks. This hybridization of falcons allowed private breeders to by-pass the economic and legal roadblocks which favored the institutional breeders and, therefore, further eroded administrative control.

While the legalization of the sale of domestic-bred falcons will result in some return to the production of pure-bred species and even perhaps of some distinctive subspecies such as Peale's falcon, it will have to be matched with a program permitting legal-permit access of private breeders to basic breeding-stock, such as white-phase gyrfalcons or Aleutian Peale's peregrine falcons, to be successful. Some breeders will no doubt continue with experiments in hybridization in attempts to produce birds with characteristics valuable to falconers. The eventual production of completely new and recognizable domestic types of falcons produced specifically for falconry seems now a certainty, just as different breeds of dogs, cats, horses and cattle have been produced. However, such new breeds of falcons will be brought into being and production much more quickly than has ever before been possible.

With the foregoing in mind, it is now possible to briefly describe and to review the six species of North American falcons formerly, and to some degree currently, available for falconry; remember many of the falcons now available from breeders may not be any of these.

AMERICAN KESTREL

10 - 12 in. (25-30 cm.) 3.85 - 4.22 oz. (109 - 119 g.)

The smallest of North American falcons, the American kestrel is brightly colored red-brown while the males also have blue-gray wings. Kestrels are about the same size and weight as mourning doves. The summer range of the kestrel includes most of the continent north to the tree-line. They often nest in tree-cavities which woodpeckers usually make and in man-made nestboxes. Their summer food is primarily insects, especially grasshoppers; their winter food is primarily mice and small birds.

A fledgling kestrel clings to a post

**American kestrel. Upper: adult male ;
lower: adult female**

Kestrels are less of a beginner falcon than a delightful pet falcon for an eight to twelve year old. Kestrels are highly individualized and most will not hunt at all once they are tamed. There is the occasional individual which makes good pursuit-flights after house sparrows and starlings. The tendency of kestrels to stall and to hover makes them difficult to train as lure-falcons.

As a group, kestrels occur world-wide with the largest number of species being found in Africa.

**Patterns of American kestrels in flight
Top: adult male; bottom: adult female**

Black merlin. Upper: adult male;
lower: adult female

MERLIN

10 - 12 in. (25 - 30 cm.) 5.3 - 7.95 oz. (150 - 225 g.)

A merlin is a small falcon which looks and measures about the same size as a kestrel, but is nevertheless one-third larger by weight. Merlins have a circumpolar breeding range best described as extending from the high mid-latitudes (north of the 40th parallel) to the low high-latitudes; that is, north to the arctic tree-line. Within this range, merlins occur most abundantly in northern savannahlands bordering grassland steppes and prairies and in arctic savannahs where the last trees fringe the arctic tundras. Merlins utilize a wide range of nesting sites; in prairie savannahs, they often use old magpie or crow nests while in spruce forests they use abandoned nests of crows, ravens, red-tailed hawks or roughleg hawks. Some ground nests are used, but they are mostly near or north of the tree-line. Most merlins are brown falcons because all first-year merlins are brown and all female merlins are brown. The males follow the pattern of the large falcons in acquiring a beautiful blue-gray plumage with the first moult and then look quite different from females and first-year birds.

Adult male black merlin

In the literature of medieval English falconry, merlins were the falcon of ladies, complete with a classic flight to the English skylark. The comparable North American quarry would be horned larks, but most merlins trained for falconry on this continent are oriented toward starlings as the main quarry because they are both abundant and legally unprotected. Also, merlins are inclined to carry small quarries, but starlings are usually large enough not to be carried far.

Merlins are also superb lure-falcons. Flown to a lightweight, starling-size lure swung from the tip of a light fiberglass pole, every stoop, outrun, dodge and aerial maneuver of a hard flight to real quarry can be duplicated with no risk of loss of the falcon. Merlins regularly flown to the lure take most field quarries with such ease and such assurance as to make the field flight the less interesting and exciting of the two.

Merlin: nest in spruce, boreal forest

Patterns of merlins in flight. Upper: adult male, common merlin; center: first-year male, common merlin; lower: adult male, black merlin.

Adult.

F.L.B.

First-year.

APLOMADO FALCON

13 - 15 in. (32.5 - 37.5 cm.)

An aplomado falcon is a medium size falcon almost exactly midway in size and in weight between merlins and peregrines. Although listed in American bird books as being a rare bird, this falcon is really a South American species and is rare only because it reaches the northern limit of its range in the extreme southwest of the United States.

This falcon, or perhaps more correctly the small group of southern-hemisphere falcons to which it belongs, is of considerable interest to falconry and to falcon breeders. Aplomado falcons are the most abundant and have the largest range of a group of southern hemisphere falcons which includes the bat falcon and orange-breasted falcon of tropical America, the New Zealand falcon and probably the brown hawk of Australia. Of these, the most interesting to falconers are the larger subspecies of aplomado falcons such as those from Chile and southern Argentina — which are prairie-falcon size — and the peregrine-size orange-breasted falcon of tropical South America — a swift and powerful falcon with oversize feet and beak which is probably the most highly-specialized raptorial bird in the world. As falconer's birds, the entire group is virtually unknown and untested, although some aplomado falcons have been trained in South America.

M.C. LEE

Adult female aplomado falcon

Prairie falcon, adult

PRAIRIE FALCON

15 - 18 in. (37.5 - 45 cm.) 525 - 980 g.

Prairie falcons are a crow-sized, sandy-brown falcon of western mid-continental North America. They are the common falcon of the complex of deserts, grasslands and arid savannahs which form the southwestern third of the continent ranging from the arid Mexican highland northward and eastward to southwestern Canada. Most of the population of prairie falcons is not migratory, although there is some southward movement of those which breed at the northern limits of their range. Prairie falcons do not construct their own nests and they do not use the abandoned tree nests of other birds. Except for one or two nestings of human-released birds on buildings, all prairie falcons nest on cliff ledges or in holes in the cliffs.

Prairie falcons are the North American counterpart of the lanner falcon of Africa and the lugger falcon of India; they are also closely related to saker falcons and gyrfalcons. Due to their easy availability and the fact much of their breeding range lies within climatic zones most favorable to human occupation, prairie falcons have become the most widely-utilized North American falcon by falconers.

Prairie falcons were the first large falcon to respond to attempts at domestication and they remain the easiest to breed in numbers. They were, accordingly, the species most successfuly hybridized, usually with gyrfalcons or peregrines, in the production of pre-1983 saleable offspring.

Head studies of a first-year prairie falcon

Prairie falcons have been trained and flown in North America for a sufficient length of time and by a sufficient number of individual falconers to prove conclusively they can be effective field-falcons. The records prove they can be trained to take most of the important field-quarries available. However, the sharp-tailed grouse and the sage grouse do seem to be two species beyond the capabilities of the prairie falcon.

The author's wife training a first-year prairie falcon

DAVID HANCOCK

Among large falcons, prairie falcons remain the most irascible and the most unforgiving in their attitude toward their trainer while in the field they are the least predictable. Although at the time this text is being written, prairie falcons or some hybrid of prairies falcons are the least expensive and the most available of all falcons, there are already indications these conditions will not last long. Due to their shortcomings in temperament and performance, there is less time and less effort going into the breeding of this species. As a breeder bird, the prairie falcon is to be by-passed, if never entirely abandoned, in favor of peregrine, gyrfalcons and saker falcons. Also, the aplomado group of falcons may come into greater use as it becomes better known to breeders. Currently the peregrine and its hybrids are the most widely utilized North American falcons.

29

Prairie falcon, adult female feeding young

K. MORCK

Peale's peregrine falcon. Left: adult female; right: adult male.

PEREGRINE FALCON

13 - 23 in. (32.5 - 57.5 cm.) 297 - 1597 g.

The extreme differences in size and weight which the above figures indicate show peregrine falcons are members of a world-wide group whose members are much alike in appearance, but are diverse in size while occupying a wide range of habitats. The tiercel of the tiny north African *F. p. minor* is the smallest peregrine, being scarcely larger than most female merlins. The largest peregrine is the female of the north pacific *F.p. pealei* which is over four times the weight of the African peregrine and is fully as large and as heavy as most male gyrfalcons. Of all the different species of animals on our planet, only humans occupy a wider range of climate and habitat than do peregrine falcons. There are no peregrine falcons in Antarctica; otherwise, at least one of the eighteen scientifically described and recognized subspecies of peregrines occurs in every other climate and region of the world. Most of these peregrines and all of the tropical and subtropical types are non-migratory. The Siberian and North American arctic peregrines are highly migratory while some of the northern mid-latitudinal peregrines also partially migrate.

Head of a first-year peregrine

DAVID HANCOCK

Beginning in the 1970s, the entire group of peregrine falcons has been internationally listed as endangered. This listing was based on the documented decline of two of the eighteen subspecies, both of which occupied regions with a high human density. These endangered subspecies are the northern European *F. p. peregrinus* and the southeastern third of the population of North American *F. p. anatum*. Both allegedly declined due to contamination with the pesticide DDT. For anyone seeking a broader understanding of the situation, the reading of *Peregrine Falcons—Their Biology and Decline* is recommended. A critical alternative to this view can be found in the last chapter of *Hawks, Falcons and Falconry* entitled "The Endangering of the Peregrine."

A captive breeding Peale's falcon at the Hancock Wildlife Research Center 1965, the world's first commercial falcon breeding project.   DAVID HANCOCK

Heads of first-year North American peregrine falcons showing main subspecific characters. Top: the Arctic peregrine f.p. tundrius, small size, pale general tone, light crown, narrow, black, broken malar stripe; center: the continental peregrine f.p. anatum, medium size, contrastingly marked; bottom: Peale's peregrine f.p. pealei, large size, dark general tone, crown and malar stripe dark grey.

Peale's peregrine aerie, Langara Island, Queen Charlotte Isle, B.C.

Peregrine and young

Peregrine falcon: an adult arctic female near the aerie

DAVID HANCOCK

Peregrines are the falcon of classic English literature. As a result, they have developed an aura of glamor in North American falconry which is not entirely warranted. If peregrines are the most-prized falcon, it is only because few contemporary falconers have any experience with gyrfalcons or sakers. In the areas of the world east of the Mediterranean where falconry has an unbroken history, peregrines are not so highly favored. At the same time, it is worth noting most of the peregrines available to falconers in these areas belong to two small subspecies known to western falconers as shaheens. North American and northern European peregrines are much larger than shaheens.

Peale's falcon: an experiment in clearing gulls from an airport

DAVID HANCOCK

Patterns of peregrine falcons in flight
Top: adult; bottom: first year

Peregrines have one behavioral characteristic which is more highly developed than in any other kind of falcon. In the disciplined flight style known to falconers as "waiting on" — where the falcon goes up above the falconer and holds this position in the air in anticipation of quarry being flushed out under it — peregrines excel. No other kind of falcon trains so easily and so naturally to this flight.

Most peregrines have an equable disposition which makes them easy to work with and a high consistency of performance once they are trained. Because breeders currently give the peregrine the most attention, they will shortly become the most easily obtained falcon. At the present time, most domestic peregrines are of mixed sub-specific ancestry. However, if access to wild-breeding stocks is made a part of the current administrative trend toward the encouragement of breeders to breed definable species and sub-species, then indeed purebred birds of such subspecies as Peale's falcon will quickly be produced.

GYRFALCONS and SAKERS

Until recently, gyrfalcons and saker falcons were treated as different species in scientific literature. They are now thought to be subtypes of a single species. The large reddish-brown, pale-headed desert falcons of Iran, Pakistan and Afghanistan, the birds contemporary Arab falconers most commonly used for hawking houbara bustard, intergrade to the north and east with slightly larger and darker-colored mountain falcons. These mountain falcons, formerly described as altai falcons, are the resident falcons of the high mountain systems of central Asia, including the Pamirs, Tien Shan Altai and Tibetan highlands. Some of these Asian highland falcons are almost indistinguishable in size and color from dark-phase gyrfalcons of southern Greenland, Labrador and the high icefield ranges of southern Alaska and the Yukon Territory.

Gyrfalcon, adult, grey phase

- Frank L. Beebe -

The red desert color-phase, known as the saker falcon, does not occur in North America. From the falconers' point of view, this is the single most important difference between gyrfalcons and sakers. On this continent, gyrfalcons have not extended their range far enough southward to have developed a similar subtype tolerant of the desert summer heat. In Asia, gyrfalcons developed from sakers. The expansion of their range was probably from south to north as they slowly followed the northward expansion of ice-free landscapes.

Immature female saker

The nearest thing to saker falcons now in North America are gyrfalcon-prairie falcon hybrids. Gyrfalcon-saker hybrids are not true species hybrids, but the birds produced from such a cross are more tolerant of warm temperatures than are most gyrfalcons.

The red-brown south Asian saker falcons have the longest history of uninterrupted use by man of any falcon or any form of wildlife in the world. They inhabit areas of the world where falconry had its origins and were probably the birds first utilized for falconry. Asian saker falcons are the sacred falcons of ancient Egypt and the "Al Hur" of contemporary Arabia. These falcons have been traditionally captured in Persia (Iran), Afghanistan and Pakistan (north-

Patterns of gyrfalcons in flight.
Upper: adult white phase; center: adult gray phase; lower: first year dark phase.

43

ern India). Thousands of these saker falcons have been sold annually for at least thirty centuries in Asian-hawk markets. However, they are still one of the world's most abundant falcons.

The far-northern falcons began as an arctic adaptation of an early saker-falcon stock, "Hur"-falcon. The name gyrfalcon is phonetically derived from the Arabic word "Hur." These northern falcons are heavier, stronger, swifter and more energetic than typical sakers. Because they occupy the largest unbroken area-range — most of which is devoid of human occupation — of any falcon, northern falcons are also the most abundant, a fact which many contemporary zoologists and administrators loathe to admit. The breeding range of gyrfalcons is usually described as being circumpolar north of the tree-line, but it is really much larger because they commonly occur and breed in mountain and highland areas in excess of a thousand miles southward of what arctic tree-line maps indicate. On this continent, gyrfalcons occupy an arctic-subarctic and mountain breeding range more than twice the size of the area prairie falcons occupy. Further, the area gyrfalcons occupy is so thinly occupied with humans that the ratio of birds to people is greater than that of prairie falcons.

Gyrfalcons range in color from white, sparingly flecked and spotted with black, through ranges of pale gray lightly barred with dark or slaty gray of the same general tone as most peregrines to such a dark smoke-gray as to appear as black as a raven unless they are viewed close at hand. While not entirely consistent with breeding range and latitude, the color of gyrfalcons is linked to latitude and point of origin in a loose kind of way. In North America, the arctic tree-line runs diagonally to the meridians northwest and southeast from the Mackenzie delta to just south of Churchill, Manitoba. Most gyrfalcons breeding northeast of the tree-line, except those of northern Quebec and Labrador and nearly all those breeding on the arctic islands, are white or nearly-white gyrfalcons. Those gyrfalcons breeding west and south of this tree-line in the sparse taiga-forest west of Hudson's Bay to the MacKenzie River are nearly all gray-phase gyrfalcons. Most gyrfalcons which breed west of the MacKenzie in the Yukon Territory, Alaska and the mountains of northern British Columbia are also gray-phase birds. The dark-colored gyrfalcons were originally described as occurring only in Labrador and southern Greenland, but it is now known almost equally dark gyrfalcons occur in the St. Elias and the Icefield ranges which front the Gulf of Alaska.

Throughout most of the history of falconry, these arctic-subarctic gyrfalcons, particularly the white birds, have been considered the ultimate falcon. They are at once the largest, most beautiful and most capable of all falcons. Contemporary evidence can support few other historic myths so well because one can certainly maintain

Gyrfalcon: A first-year grey-phase female ALBERTA GOVERNMENT

most gyrfalcons, if properly trained and given the chance to prove themselves in the field, live up to their historical and their mythical reputations. For the contemporary falconer, these gyrfalcons have only two shortcomings as an ideal falconry bird. One of these, already mentioned, is their inability to perform well in warm climates. The other is the difficulty, and with some individuals the impossibility, of persuading them about the advantage gained by going aloft and "waiting on" over the falconer. This last short-coming was not the fault of ancient falconry as we shall presently see. Otherwise, gyrfalcons today hold their "pride of place" as the ultimate falcon as well as they ever have.

Goshawk

Hawks

In the published writings about birds of contemporary North America—much of which are published in scientific journals—hawks receive less than one-tenth the attention and the research grants which are given falcons. Somehow, the use of hawks as trained hunting birds is considered to be of little importance and they do not give rise to anything approaching the emotional overtones which have marked the similar use of falcons. This current elitist attitude at both scientific and administrative levels is so obvious and pronounced that it suggests some kind of lingering influence of medieval northern European attitudes when ownership of falcons was confined to the nobility while the use of hawks was not. It may be worth further comment that this curious emotional attitude concerning falcons remains almost entirely confined to people of north European origin. Elsewhere, across Asia from Turkey to Japan—except on the Arabian peninsula—goshawks were the most prized of hunting hawks. For example, Japanese hawking was almost entirely confined to the use of this one species.

A current anomaly which is part of contemporary falconry results from scientific and administrative over-regulation of falcons. Despite the restricted access of falconers to wild falcon population, these birds have—through domestication—become more available through purchase than most hawks are through permit.

Of the six kinds of North American forest (accipiter) and savannah (buteo) hawks which have proved useful as falconers' birds, only the Harris's hawk has become reasonably available from breeders. Most of the others have been domestic-bred, but only on an experimental basis. Hybridization has been mostly confined to red-tail crosses with Harris's hawks but has recently expanded to include other hawks.

One of the more interesting aspects of North American hawking is only two of the six kinds of native North American hawks currently in use have Eurasion counterparts. The use of goshawks and sparrowhawks is ancient and widespread, but Cooper's hawks, red-tailed hawks, ferruginous hawks and Harris's hawks are new to hawking and to hawking literature. Almost everything concerning them and absolutely everything published about them as falconers' birds has been learned in only twenty years. At the present time, five of these six species are only available to falconers with regionally issued state, provincial or territorial wildlife acquisition and holding permits. These permits allow a falconer to use the bird, but the state retains nominal ownership. In the United States these are joint state and federal permits while in Canada these are provincial or territorial permits only. Under this permit system, most applicants almost continent-wide can legally obtain one or two of the six worthwhile species. Over most of the United States, the two species for which permits are most readily obtained are Cooper's hawks and red-tailed hawks. In Canada, the most readily-obtained species are goshawks and red-tailed hawks. Some regional administrations in both countries still refuse to honor all non-institutional applications.

As huntsmen's hawks, the six species about to be reviewed can be classified into two distinct types. Three are forest hawks (accipiters) of which two American species — goshawk and sharp-shinned hawk — are the American counterparts of the Eurasian goshawks and sparrowhawks of ancient and classic falconry. The third American accipiter, Cooper's hawk, is new to falconry and has proven to be different from the other two accipiters because it requires slightly different handling and training techniques. The other three — red-tailed hawk, ferruginous hawk and Harris's hawk — are American savannahland hawks. These hawks are closely related, but they are strikingly different in appearances, mannerisms and hunting styles. All three hawks are new to falconry.

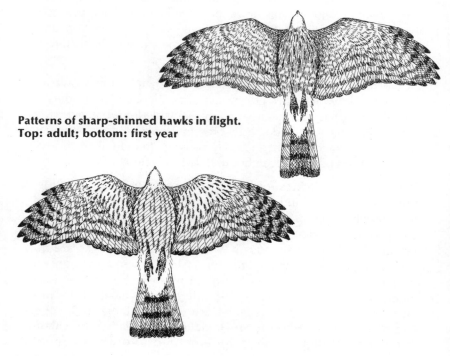

**Patterns of sharp-shinned hawks in flight.
Top: adult; bottom: first year**

SHARP-SHINNED HAWK

10 - 12 in. (10.2 - 12.2 cm.) 3.6 - 6.4 oz. (102 - 179 g.)

Sharp-shinned hawks are about the same size and weight as kestrels and are the smallest American hawk regularly trained for hunting. In apparent size and color and in the types of quarries they seek, they are similar to merlins. Like merlins, the first-moult color change from brown to blue-gray is confined to males. Most sharp-shinned hawks are colored brown, including all females and all first-year birds.

**Sharp-shinned hawk: Nest in spruce,
boreal forest**

Sharp-shinned hawks breed continent-wide from Mexico northward to the tree-line. Thus, they have a breeding range comparable in size only to red-tailed hawks and kestrels. The northern-breeding birds are highly migratory as many fly the length of the continent to winter in the American tropics. If the sharp-shinned hawk is not the most abundant of North American hawks and falcons, its only rival is the kestrel.

Sharp-shinned hawks are only one of at least thirty kinds of small forest hawks with a world-wide distribution known collectively as sparrowhawks. Of these, the species best known to falconry are those which naturally occur in the areas of the world where they have been traditionally used. The sparrowhawk (*a nisus*) of English and northern European literature is the best known, followed by the shikra, levant and besra sparrowhawks of the area extending eastward from the Mediterranean to India. All are much alike: about the same size, abundant enough to be easily captured and easily trained.

If it is no longer true these small hawks are currently the most-widely captured and utilized of all the birds of falconry, they once were. They had their highest value and utility throughout the area east of the Mediterranean because they served as the least expensive and most effective method of catching the migratory coturnix quail. In other areas, such as northern India and medieval Europe, sharp-shinned hawks were a kind of everyman's hawk as their use varied from utilitarian to recreational.

Young sharp-shinned hawks

North American sharp-shinned hawks are no different from their Eurasian counterparts. They are abundant and easily captured — however, it is easier to obtain the bird than it is to obtain the necessary permit. Considering they are accipiters, these birds are easily trained, but on this continent they are not a commonly-used hawk. The quarries they hunt best are small insectivorous songbirds, nearly all of which are internationally protected in North America. Trained sharp-shinned hawks capture house-sparrows and starlings with ease if a close approach can be made. If they could be captured, trained and flown for a short autumn season and then released in the eastern-Mediterranean tradition, without permits and without official interference, they might receive more attention. With current official attitudes and restrictions, though, they are scarcely worth the trouble. Most birds used in North American falconry must be retained longer than one season to justify the imposed problems.

Banded sharp-shinned hawk just before being released

Adult North American goshawk

GOSHAWK

20 - 27 in. (22.4 - 26.4 cm.) 20 - 75 oz. (560 - 2054 g.)

Goshawks are the largest, strongest and swiftest of the forest hawks (accipiters). These big hawks, together with sakers, gyrfalcons and peregrines, belong to the group of raptor species associated with humans at the dawn of history. It could be said humans rode out of the darkness of pre-history astride a horse with a goshawk or a saker on their left hands.

Patterns of goshawks in flight. Top: adult; bottom: first year

First year North American goshawk

European Goshawk

JOHN BURCHARD

Northern goshawks are cool or cold-climate birds with a circumpolar range primarily in the belt of coniferous forest which encircles the northern continents just south of the polar barrens. This range extends southward in highlands and high-elevation mountain forests. In North America, this southern extension reaches northern Mexico and similar latitudes in Eurasia. However, some of the European and Asian highland populations are discontinuous with, and isolated from, the northern European trans-Siberian population.

Except for the pale sometimes-white *albidus* subspecies of north-eastern Siberia and Kamchatka, the other eight listed subspecies of northern goshawks are much alike in appearance, but somewhat different in size. The birds from northern Germany and Scandinavia are the largest goshawks. These, along with the slightly paler buteoides from Finland and adjacent northern European Russia, are the goshawks which have received the most attention from breeders, mostly because of their large size. Exceptionally large North American goshawks almost match the average European birds in measurements and weight, but never in the size and the strength of their feet. These are the only really constant and significant differences between North American and European goshawks.

CECIL CLARK

When they are competently trained, handled and regularly taken afield, goshawks remain as much the ultimate hawk as gyrfalcons are the ultimate falcon. In some ways, they excell all other raptors as a huntsman's bird. Goshawks can take a wider range of difficult quarries over a wider range of climate, weather and terrain than

Goshawk nest in aspen

any other kind of hawk or falcon. They train equally well as nestlings, brown passage hawks or gray adults. Traditionally, from ancient times until the late-medieval period, few goshawks were taken from nests, but the reverse is now the case, especially in Europe and North America.

In the ancient traditional falconry of Turkey, central Asia, Persia, Pakistan (northern India) and Japan, goshawks were, and still are in some of these areas, the ultimate and the most-valued hunting hawks. In North America, while recognized as the swiftest and most competent hawk species in comparison with red-tailed hawks or Harris's hawks, goshawks are also known to be difficult hawks to obtain and to train. They have a reputation for becoming easily lost under field conditions and they are difficult to maintain free of disease. All of these difficulties concerning goshawks have some validity, but they all apply more to American goshawks than to Eurasian birds.

In the northern spruce-forests, across Canada and southward in the high-elevation conifer woods of the western mountains, goshawks are the most abundant of the large hawks. The difficulties North American falconers now encounter in obtaining these birds are entirely imposed and related to permits, regional administrative policies and political boundaries. Perhaps the current situation, as it applies to goshawks, best illustrates the degree to which political considerations, not scientific research, have control over North American administrative management of hawks and falcons.

Until the late 1960s, goshawks were on the vermin lists of every state, provincial and territorial administration north of Mexico and, as a result, they could be destroyed anywhere. Also, goshawks could be captured, retained and transported anywhere on the continent or to any part of the world. However, until the late 1960s, the organizations which held political control of wildlife administrators were regional hunting and fishing clubs.

Goshawks are now as abundant and as destructive to game birds and to poultry as they were then, but now they are nationally protected in the United States and regionally protected in all Canadian wildlife administrative regions. Some Canadian jurisdictions issue resident capture permits, but none issue non-resident permits. These changes are entirely political since they result from the contemporary influence of regional environmentalist and bird-watcher clubs backed by international nature protection organizations. It is curious that while all Canadian wildlife administrations issue permits which allow, or even advertise, for non-resident hunters to come into their jurisdictions to kill rare wildlife, such as mountain sheep, mountain goats,

First year European goshawk. Damaged feathers of the tail have been replaced (imped) with those from a snowy owl

grizzly bears and caribou, none allow non-residents to capture goshawks.

Since this current situation, which involves not just goshawks but all raptors, is entirely political, it is subject to change — such a change would be to the economic advantage of northern wildlife administrations. Should non-resident permits become available from any of the far-northern administrations from Newfoundland to Alaska, there is one more observation which can be made regarding North American goshawks. Simply stated, the farther north a goshawk originates, the better the bird it is likely to be as a falconer's hawk. There is no explanation for this observation, but goshawks captured in autumn on the rim of the arctic are so different in behavior from mid-latitude goshawks that they may as well be a different species. These northern goshawks can be tamed and trained more easily than red-tails and, once trained, they are the most spirited and the most competent of goshawks. Therefore, they are well worth going far north to obtain should they ever again become legally available to falconers.

Cooper's hawk, adult

COOPER'S HAWK

15 - 20 in. (15.2 - 25.6 cm.) 13.4 - 19.8 oz. (380 - 560 g.)

Cooper's hawks are a North American mid-latitude forest hawk (accipiter) almost exactly midway in size between sharp-shinned hawks and goshawks. They are one of a group of four North American hawks which have no comparable counterparts in the lands of ancient or classic falconry. As a result, their use as falconers's birds spans only thirty years and, except for a few birds exported to England and Germany before 1970, experience with them is confined entirely to North America.

Patterns of Cooper's hawks in flight: Top: adult; bottom: first year.

Cooper's hawk: Typical nest in a maple

The breeding range of Cooper's hawks is continent-wide, but it is concentrated in the mid-latitude United States. Accordingly, the breeding range superimposes over the same part of the continent most densely occupied and changed by human activity. Although a true forest hawk, Cooper's hawks prefer patch-forests over continuous forest. Human activities which change large forest tracts to meadows, fields and patch-forests greatly favor the requirements of this hawk.

First-year Cooper's hawks look almost like small goshawks in color and markings. Like goshawks, Cooper's hawks change from brown to blue-gray with the first moult, but they are crossbarred with reddish-brown on all undersurfaces during adulthood and, as a result they are quite distinctive. On a continental basis, Cooper's hawks are probably less numerous than goshawks. Their total range is smaller than that of goshawks and little of it is wilderness. Nevertheless, their more southerly range and their casual adaptability to occupation of human-altered landscapes make Cooper's hawks the most available forest hawk for American falconers. In addition, because all American bird books list Cooper's hawks as common birds and goshawks as rare, there have been few political problems associated with obtaining permits for Cooper's hawks.

This dual availability of permits and of birds has made Cooper's hawks the most widely utilized of the North American forest hawks. However, the nature of the birds themselves prevents them from ever becoming popular with falconers. Despite their adaptation to human-occupied landscapes and their unconcerned acceptance of human activities, wild-caught Cooper's hawks have proven to be so intractable and so fearful that all attempts to do anything with them have been abandoned. It is only when they are taken as nestlings and brought to flying age in association with people that Cooper's hawks are effective and are rewarding birds for falconry. Given this pre-condition, they have proven themselves on a wide range of quarries, from starlings and feral pigeons to small cottontails, pheasant poults and pond ducks. The best flights of Cooper's hawks are to quail because they pursue quail with a greater intensity than they show for any other kind of quarry. Any falconer who lives in an area where any of the several kinds of American quail are abundant enough to provide regular legal open-hunting seasons must at least consider trying a Cooper's hawk.

Adult Cooper's hawk with nearly fledged young

K. MORCK

RED-TAILED HAWK

22 - 25 in. (22.4 - 25.4 cm.) 36.3 - 43.2 oz. (1,028 - 1,224 g.)

Red-tails are a large North American mid-latitude sparse forest or savannahland hawk. It is the most abundant and easily seen of all the larger North American raptorial birds. The breeding range of the red-tailed hawk is essentially the same as those of sharp-shinned hawks and kestrels or equal to the combined ranges of Cooper's Hawks and goshawks. The northern half of the breeding population is migratory.

Head study of a fledgling red-tailed hawk

K. MORCK

Patterns of red-tailed hawks in flight. Upper: western red-tail, (a) first year, (b) adult; lower: Harlan's red-tail, (a) first year, (b) adult.

All red-tailed hawks are brown hawks throughout their life. As the name indicates, most adult red-tailed hawks have a tail colored in some shade of bright brick-red. However, all first-year red-tailed hawks do not have red tails. Systematic zoologists list fourteen different races or subspecies of this hawk, all slightly different in size and in appearance from different parts of the continent. The two types of hawks most difficult to recognize as red-tailed hawks are some of the white-tailed birds from Montana and western Alberta which belong to the Krider's hawk (kriderii) subspecies and some of the dark-colored birds with tails marbled in an inter-mingled complex of brown, white and red-brown from the migratory northwest population which breeds in the Yukon Territory and Alaska and belongs to the Harlan's hawk (harlani) subspecies.

In measurements and in weight, goshawks and red-tailed hawks are similar, but red-tails have larger wings and shorter tails than goshawks. The largest red-tails are non-migratory birds from the oak-savannahs of the eastern and midwestern United States. These red-tails easily match the largest European goshawks in weight and in strength. The smallest red-tails are the southern insular sub-species like those from Jamaica, and the dark-colored forest red-tails of the Pacific Northwest Coast.

Unlike goshawks and Cooper's hawks, which are secretive and may be common birds without being seen, red-tailed hawks are highly visible. They spend much of their time soaring. Also, red-tails often scream at one another while aloft and so draw attention. They perch, through preference, on high-exposed poles, posts or dead trees; their nests are large and unconcealed. The fact a bird so large, so obvious and so easily approached has been able to survive a full century of vermin or bounty status and continue to be abundant indicates the biological resilience these raptors have.

Prior to and since their continent-wide protection, red-tails have been the most-easily obtained of the larger hawks. Being a common hawk found continent-wide and having no monetary trade value, falconers's use of red-tails has aroused no concern. Wherever the capture of hawks is permitted, permits for this species are usually available. As a huntsman's hawk, red-tails are restricted to flights to ground quarries, usually rabbits or hares. Red-tails are not successful as bird-hawks, although the odd individual may learn how to catch pheasants on the ground. As with Cooper's hawks, the use of red-tails has no historic background and the total experience with them covers less than thirty years; this experience is almost entirely confined to North America.

Except for Harris's hawks, red-tails are the most easily and completely tameable of all hawks or falcons; this characteristic holds true whether they are taken as nestlings or any time later. Many of these red-tails, but especially those taken as nestlings, form a strong attachment to their trainer and to a home territory. Birds which make this dual attachment are not easily lost. Red-tails also live a long time and are exceedingly tough and disease resistant. While these characteristics may seem to be all which would most recommend red-tails as a beginner's hawk, the novice should be warned getting free of one may become a larger problem than obtaining one. As a falconer's bird, a red-tail is not a versatile hawk and, after a couple years of experience with one, an aspiring falconer tends to attempt to expand his experience through working with more exciting birds. A further tendency, after obtaining another bird, is to release the red-tail with the hope it will return to the wild. However, releasing a tamed red-tail does not make it go away. Even taking it many miles away from its home territory before its release does not ensure it will not return. The trouble is if a red-tail does return to what it considers its home territory and finds another hawk or falcon of any kind tethered there, it will attack and kill the intruding bird if possible. Giving the red-tail to another falconer within a hundred miles of the original home territory is also not a safe thing to do. Tame red-tails are not easy to give away — zoos or animal parks do not value or even want them. This keep-*it*-or-*kill*-it characteristic of many red-tailed hawks is one of the most unexpected long-term problems novices encounter when they acquire a red-tail as their first hawk.

Eastern red-tailed hawk; adult and young

CHRIS REES

Red-tails readily reproduce in captivity. However, because the young which are produced are difficult even to give away, no source of domestic-bred red-tails has been developed or seems likely to be developed. Through the 1960s and 1970s, red-tails were the most-commonly kept and the most-commonly utilized of all North American raptors. Today, their use is rapidly declining and they are being displaced with one of the following two species. As we shall see, there is good reason for this change.

FERRUGINOUS HAWK

22 - 27 in. (22.4 - 27.6 cm.) 35 - 76 oz. (970 - 2500 g.)

The largest and the heaviest of North American hawks are the ferruginous hawks. In measurements, they are not greatly different from red-tailed hawks, but they have heavier bodies with a higher wing-loading. Also, the difference in size between the sexes is greater than in red-tails. Ferruginous hawks are birds of the short-grass savannahs, prairies, arid badlands and deserts of the western United States with a breeding range which superimposes almost exactly that of prairie falcons. As with prairie falcons, no subspecies of ferruginous hawks are known, but there are three color variations: a dark brown phase, a rusty-red phase and an almost-white phase. About eighty per cent of the total population are almost-white phase birds which greatly resemble the equally pale Krider's red-tail in color and dimensions.

A nest full of nearly fledged young

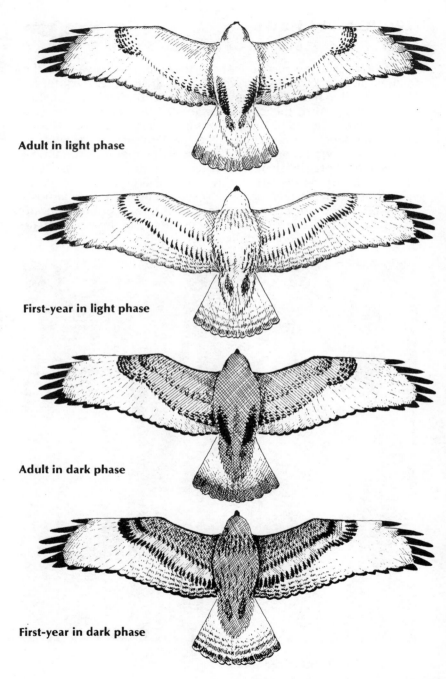

Adult in light phase

First-year in light phase

Adult in dark phase

First-year in dark phase

Patterns of ferruginous hawks in flight

TOM WILLOCK
Ground nest of ferruginous hawk on the rim of a coulee

Ferruginous hawks have a specialized reproductive requirement which limits their breeding territory to the western American plains and desert conditions. Their nests are always built near a colony of one of several different daytime-active colonial ground squirrel species; the young of these hawks are fed little else. These squirrels go underground for prolonged periods of hibernation which vary from five to seven months depending on the latitude or the aridity of the land. During this time, the squirrels are totally unavailable as food. Ferruginous hawks make abrupt changes in their food species and their hunting habits in order to adapt to the disappearance of the abundant food supply on which their young depend. This adaptation is to pursue larger and more active quarries. Primarily, their hunting capabilities are focussed on the large plains and desert hares, but they also pursue some kinds of birds. The ability of ferruginous hawks to engage in long-distance, active pursuit of these large quarries makes them interesting for falconers.

The most-successfully trained ferruginous hawks have been taken as nestlings while wild-caught individuals have a reputation for being intractable. They have been captive bred on an experimental basis, but they are not available from breeders. Young ferruginous hawks, when they are downies or are partly feathered, are so much like young red-tailed hawks in appearance and in apparent size that novices often mistake them for red-tailed hawks and use red-tail permits. Few novices and fewer wildlife officials can distinguish between them. In areas where the two occur together, it is ferruginous hawks, especially their huge nests, which are the more obvious of the two hawks.

Ferruginous hawks are in every way as tough, disease resistant and long-lived as red-tails. While novices have successfully trained some, ferruginous hawks are still not a good beginner's hawk. Though they are swifter in flight and considerably more spirited than red-tails, they do not have the same even-tempered disposition and they can be difficult to control. In addition, ferruginous hawks can become as territorially jealous as red-tails; ferruginous hawks are then considerably more dangerous because of their larger size and their tendency to sometimes attack strange people, dogs or other raptors.

Ferruginous hawks, nevertheless, have a valid and a useful place in American falconry because they are so similar to golden eagles and because they eliminate the need for eagles to make flights to swift hares or jackrabbits across open plains and deserts. In addition, they give interesting and sometimes effective flights to some large bird quarries of open landscapes; on these flights, they are more effective than eagles. Ferruginous hawks fly much faster than any red-tail and they cope with strong winds almost as casually as falcons. They are strictly an open-country hawk which will not enter woods or dense cover of any kind in pursuit of prey. Ferruginous hawks give North American falconers the opportunity to experience the nearest possible equivalent of hunting with eagles, but this experience is reasonably free of the risk of injury which working with golden eagles always entails.

Adult ferruginous hawk

First-year female

Adult male

HARRIS'S HAWK

20 - 24 in. (50 - 60 cm.) 20 - 70 oz. (560 - 2000 g.)

The Harris's hawk is a dark-brown, long-tailed hawk with almost exactly the same proportions, measurements, size and weight as American goshawks. Harris's hawks are totally different in appearance and in color from all other North American hawks or falcons. The head of the Harris's hawk is smaller than other hawks of similar size and it is a miniature replica of a golden eagle head. Harris's hawks have a tail which is black with a wide white tip and a white base. Their body plumage is dark brown as are their eyes. These hawks have long tarsi and large, strong, heavily armed feet. The foot size, relative to the size of the bird, is similar to that of European goshawks.

Harris's hawks, while listed in all bird books as being native to the United States, are really a South American species which, like Aplomado falcons, has extended its range northward through Central America and Mexico and into the extreme southwest of the United States. In 1964, writing in *North American Falconry and Hunting Hawks*, I drew the attention of southwestern American falconers to the possible use of Harris's hawks as follows:

"Harris's hawk (Parabuteo). This is single species of aberrant buteoine hawk of tropical origin that has penetrated into the (north) temperate zone a little farther north than the Mexican border. We do not know this bird at all well and have seen but one living specimen. It is a large hawk approaching a red-tail in size but with the proportions of an accipiter and, if the published accounts of its behavior are at all accurate, the hunting ability of the accipiters as well. Here is a species that would appear to be well worth some very serious attention for falconers wishing to fly a large goshawk-type of hunting hawk in regions where the summer temperatures go too high for birds of northern origin. Harris's hawk is apparently reasonably abundant and not too difficult to obtain either by trapping or from the nest. It appears to be as easily tamed as the red-tail. It is not a proven species at all, but one of the lesser-known of American hawks that should be given a fair trial."

Two decades later, Harris's hawks have had a fair trial. Those American falconers who gave them this trial must receive credit for making these hawks the most remarkable of all contemporary contributions to falconry.

While Harris's hawks closely resemble goshawks in measurements, weight and proportion, the similarity ends there. Everything else about them is different: color, appearance, behavior and mannerisms. These differences in behavior and mannerisms were initially surprising, but they make the Harris's hawk the most

79

adaptable and the most reliable of all hawks under the conditions of contemporary falconry.

Most raptorial birds, including all accipiters, hunt individually. Co-operative hunting, even among mated pairs in other species, is unusual, but it does happen with golden eagles, gyrfalcons and peregrines. Harris's hawks, alone among the raptors, have extended co-operative hunting as they hunt not merely in pairs, but as social groups in much the same manner as wolves. It may seem strange the co-operative group hunting patterns we have come to associate with mammals should have also developed in only one kind of hawk. However, the fact this occurrence should result in a hawk which is naturally pre-adapted to domestication and to cooperative hunting with a human partner is certainly not surprising. Also, it is not surprising, as word spread about this new kind of hawk that behaves more like a dog than a bird, Harris's hawks quickly became the most interesting and the most valued North American hunting hawks.

Before listing some of the more interesting and novel game-flights which have been accomplished with Harris's hawks, it must be made clear, however co-operative and versatile they have proven to be, they still have their limitations. Harris's hawks have short, round-tipped wings and a long tail similar to forest hawks. Like these hawks, Harris's hawks can build rapid speed in accelerating

Adult female Harris's hawk   G.M. BRANDON

Adult male Harris's hawk

M.C. LEE

flight for short distances. In this respect, and in their willingness and their ability to pursue quarries in thickets and woodlands, they resemble goshawks and Cooper's hawks more than they resemble red-tailed hawks. Nevertheless, these true accipiters are capable of swifter and more enduring pursuit than any Harris's hawk. It is also unlikely any falconer will ever see a Harris's hawk fly for half a mile or more straight into a cold wind blowing across a frozen prairie to overtake and to course a bounding jackrabbit as a ferruginous hawk can do. However, under the overall conditions which tend to govern contemporary hawking, anyone flying a Harris's hawk is likely to attain a much higher seasonal score of game, a wider variety of game and less repetition in the way game is taken than with any other kind of hawk or falcon. These results can be achieved because Harris's hawks, though they may lack any physical or aerial superiority, make up for these shortcomings in the close and cunning ways they learn to work with their human co-hunters.

The social nature of Harris's hawks, like that of dogs, is so advanced they make a stronger bond to their human hunting partner than to their home territory. At all times, they seem to recognize other Harris's hawks as being of their own kind and they seldom show either jealousy or aggression toward strange individuals. Harris's hawks are the safest of all hawks to fly in groups. On successful flights, much more than any other kind of hawk, Harris's hawks look for and expect assistance following a strike on large quarry. Perhaps they become extremely courageous in attacking things outside their size range because they quickly learn such assistance is always forthcoming. Following unsuccessful flights, Harris's hawks become as concerned with locating and with returning to their human partner as the human is concerned with finding the hawk. Therefore, the use of Harris's hawks is free of any worry of losing the bird; they are the only hawks which can be regularly flown in the field without the use of bells or telemetry transmitters.

With such a willingly co-operative hawk, some innovative ways of bringing them within range of their quarries have been successful. These innovative methods include: carrying the hawk unhooded and unrestrained in a slow-moving automobile while positioning the bird to fly out the right-hand window after any ditch or roadside quarries — rabbits, pheasants, waterfowl, crows or starlings — and being able to call the hawk back through the same window if the flight fails; group-hawking — use ferrets to force colonial burrowing mammals, such as ground-squirrels and European rabbits, from their burrows before simultaneously releasing eight or ten Harris's hawks to the one quarry without any risk to the hawks; "waiting on" stoop-flights where wind and hill conditions permit the hawks to slope-soar over the falconer; night-hawking — spotlighting rabbits or rats in darkness and similarly spotlighting a lure on the ground or a gloved hand in order to retrieve the hawk at night.

Harris's hawks have proven to be as willing and as co-operative in domestic reproduction as they have been in other ways. They are the only kind of hawk which receives the same amount of attention breeders give falcons — with two small, but perhaps significant, differences. These differences are most Harris's hawks being produced are the result of hobby breeding and equally significant, this species, being a hawk and not a falcon, has received no attention from institutional breeders, even though it is rarer in the United States and in Canada than gyrfalcons or peregrine falcons.

Game, Vermin, Predators and Wildlife

The complex of regional, federal and international regulations and permit restrictions pertaining to the capture, keeping, breeding, transporting or shipping of falcons and hawks which currently constrains North American and European falconry was imposed over a period of less than five years in the late 1960s and early 1970s. None of these regulations or restrictions are the least bit necessary and all are fraudulent to the extent they really do nothing to protect hawks and falcons. This complex serves only as a disguise because it really serves to protect special privileges or to further the political goals of organized international groups promoting new environmental and wildlife-protection philosophies. To a considerable degree, peregrine falcons and gyrfalcons are used as bellwethers to set regional and international regulatory precedents. Thus, they test public acceptance or public indifference to some new and, once the implications are realized, some alarming professional and international wildlife administration concepts.

For the reader to understand the implications of some of the current professional attitudes toward falconry and falconers, and the expression of these as administrative experiments, a review of the evolution of European and of North American ideas and attitudes about game, vermin, predators and wildlife is required.

North American attitudes toward birds of prey have undergone profound change over the past half century and have moved as far from one extreme to another as it is possible to imagine. During the 1920s and early 1930s, all birds of prey in every province and state on the North American continent were officially classified as *vermin*. At times, they were not merely vermin, but they were bountied vermin. This distinction meant public funds were appropriated to purchase some specific part, usually the feet, of dead raptors, the idea being such payment would encourage the public to kill all hawks and all owls. Usually, no attempt was made to identify species, but when there was, eagles and bird-eating hawks — goshawks, Cooper's hawks, peregrine falcons, prairie falcons and gyrfalcons — were the species always listed as being particularly vile and deserving of speedy extermination.

Abruptly in 1970, this distinction, as far as official policy was concerned, was completely reversed. In that year, both in Canada and in the United States, public funds were appropriated to be spent on domestic propagation programs designed to *save from*

threatened extinction some of the same species — golden eagle, bald eagle, peregrine falcon, gyrfalcon and prairie falcon — which twenty years earlier had been drawing bounties and less than a year earlier had been listed as vermin.

If the vermin status and the bountied extermination campaigns of the earlier eras now seem somewhat ugly and medieval, and the use of public funds for bounties not in the public interest, the possibility must also be entertained that the extreme opposite attitude of the 1970s — spending public funds for protection and propagation — may be equally suspect.

This swing of the pendulum of official attitude toward birds of prey is a phenomenon curiously confined to societies of northern Europe and North America and is of common and relatively recent historic origin.

Historically on a world scale, birds of prey have aroused the interest and often the admiration of people, but the attitude of most people toward them has been one of indifference. These birds, nevertheless were important to many tribes and cultures at different times and at different places as totemic or religious symbols or as symbols of status and ceremony. Often considerable time and considerable effort were expended to obtain their feathers, feet, claws or other parts. The eagle feather headdresses of the American Plains Indians are a good example of this usage. The capture or death of a bird of prey for such purposes held no overtones of the omnipotence of mankind, rather the contrary. The human, in such cases, perceived the spirit of the bird as possessing powers beyond his own; he envied these powers and he attempted to make them available to himself through the symbolic possession of some part of the bird.

The only other significant interest humans, other than those of northern European origin, took in these birds was in the capture of individuals of some species for training in a co-operative hunting partnership. Where falconry flourished, particularly in those parts of the world where it became traditional, the human attitude toward these birds was benign. The companionate use of birds of prey among societies which had no background of hostility toward them had no adverse effect on their wild populations. Under these circumstances, the capture and the taming of an individual bird exposed it to no danger from other humans even when it escaped the custody of its trainer. Consequently, birds of prey are both abundant and unafraid in parts of the world such as Arabia, Pakistan, India and Turkey where their capture, sale and use has an uninterrupted tradition of thousands of years.

Golden eagle, first year

The evolution of ideas took a different course in Europe. In Europe, ideas concerning non-human life developed against the background of a deeply-entrenched class system expressed in the medieval ideas of hereditary, manorial land ownership as integrated with the Judeo-Christian religious and ethical dogma. Any system of thought which at once accepts and promotes as self-evident the divine ordainment of kings and of nobles to rule lesser men has no problem in accepting the even more self-evident parallel that men are the divinely-ordained lords, owners, overseers wardens and ultimate custodians of all other living things.

Once this basic religiously-derived attitude, unique to societies of northern European derivation, is defined, the development of the concept of vermin and the application of vermin status to birds of prey across northern Europe, the North American continent north of Mexico and Australia is not difficult to trace. Medieval thinking extended the concept of criminal culpability to animals as well as men; animals were regularly tried and regularly sentenced in medieval courts. Medieval society also made wealth and rank attributes of land ownership. Accordingly, the hunting of game produced on the land was the special privilege of the land-owning class. These ideas, codified in medieval law, made the wildlife occurring on an estate the property of the estate owner. Only the landowner, his family or his guests had any right to hunt or kill such game. In medieval thinking, therefore, to hunt uninvited on the landowner's property was a crime and any such hunter, whether man, beast or bird, was clearly a thief.

As long as birds of prey were allies of the landowner and assisted, as did trained falcons in early medieval times, in the taking of game, they were greatly esteemed. However, as firearms began to displace them, wild birds of prey began to be regarded first as a competitor and then, inevitably, as a poacher or a thief. Gamekeeping, which developed alongside the rise in popularity of sport shooting on European estates, firmly established the concept of the predator as a vile poacher.

Then followed the era of the professional gamekeeper. Throughout England and much of Europe, most of the time and the effort of professional gamekeepers was devoted to the elimination of predators which interfered with or appeared to interfere with the *keeping* of game. Eventually, vermin came to include almost everything alive which was not considered fit to eat.

Traditionally, these gamekeepers kept a gibbet, upon which were hung the carcasses of the mammal and the bird criminals which fell to an array of traps, set guns, snares, deadfalls, hooks and poisons for public display in the finest medieval style.

Settlers from northern Europe transplanted this concept of the predator as a poaching criminal to be hunted and killed on sight as an unquestioned doctrine in North America, Australia and New Zealand. The idea was modified just enough to make it fit the pioneer conditions in which hunting was not a special privilege, but it was a public right; otherwise, nothing was changed. On continents rich in both game and predators, the idea of the predator as a criminal had few critics. In keeping with the new-world concept in which game belonged to everyone, the old-world gamekeeper soon metamorphosed into a uniformed public servant — the game warden. Traditionally, one of the primary duties of the game warden was to carry on, in the European gamekeeping tradition, the destruction of all predatory vermin which might kill public game. Thus, not only in North America, but also in all the British colonies, the basic concept of gamekeeping continued to flourish. However, instead of functioning on a patchy, private scale, it was enlarged to operate on the scale of a state, province or territory. For over two centuries, this expanded version of European gamekeeping, complete with state-subsidized vermin destruction, was fundamental to game preservation policies everywhere in North America north of Mexico.

The opposite attitude is of more recent origin. During the late 1920s and the early 1930s, it became widely known migrating hawks could be killed by the thousands in certain places if wind and weather conditions were right. The two places where this kind of shooting reached levels which eventually resulted in revulsion and reaction were at Hawk Mountain in Pennsylvania and at Cape May in New Jersey; however, by the 1930s, autumn hawk shoots had become a part of the North American sport shooting tradition and were annual events wherever hawks were found to be concentrated during migration. The fanatical dedication necessary to stop this practice, fully matching and eventually exceeding that of the most ardent hawkslayer, is the subject of a book, *Hawks Aloft*, by Maurice Broun (1968), who was the first keeper of what is now the Hawk Mountain Sanctuary which is now virtually a preservationists shrine. Thus, by the late 1930s, the polarities of attitude had been defined.

The hawk destroyers, with the gamekeeping tradition as their historical rationale, viewed birds of prey as poachers and themselves as voluntary game wardens who brought well-deserved summary execution to such criminals. The protectionists viewed hawks as ravaged innocents, the victims of a gang of murderers whose bloodlust knew no bounds, and viewed themselves as altruistic protectors of the innocent.

This kind of entrenched stalemate endured virtually unchanged for twenty years. During that time, except in the sanctuaries, the raptorial birds continued to be shot, poletrapped, bountied and scientifically collected. As many as twenty thousand golden eagles were destroyed in Texas alone (Spofford, 1964).

Characteristically, the proponents of both extreme positions took remarkably little real interest in the birds of prey except as symbols and many of the most-zealous hawk protectors, like their counterparts the zealous hawk shooters, knew little about these birds. Despite their entrenched animosity and hatred for one another, these people were really only screaming different interpretations of the same basic divinely-ordained nature-custodian concept.

When the real changes came, they came from new directions. Biologists, bringing with them the evolutionary rather than the religious viewpoint, began to penetrate and to modify regional game administrative decisions in the mid-1930s. At first, they were met with suspicion and sometimes hostility, but their influence following World War Two completely changed the orientation of most regional game departments across the continent. This change was reflected in departmental name changes which largely eliminated the word *game* because the new concept of wildlife management was different from that of game preservation. While the principles of wildlife management, with their stress on habitat improvement and recreational use rather than enforcement and vermin control, have been primarily applied to the traditional game species. However, whether they are applied or not, they are valid for other species as well. Wildlife management recognized the role of predators in natural wildlife systems and with this recognition came the end of most organized, state-sponsored predator control programs, including those designed to eliminate raptorial birds.

It was this change in attitude toward predatory species generally, as a logical result of wildlife management concepts at the regional level, which brought about this change in management. The further innovation of regional regulatory or protective statutes specifically designed for the birds of prey was quite a different matter. Generally speaking, they remained in a kind of statutory limbo, neither protected, regulated, nor officially persecuted during the decade of the 1950s. During this hiatus, North American falconry achieved a surge of growth and interest. *North American Falconry and Hunting Hawks* was published in 1960. I cannot believe it was altogether just coincidence that regional statutory attention specific to birds of prey was virtually complete continent-wide by 1965. Now, while protectionist organizations such as Audubon certainly urged this kind of regional attention, the efforts of regional wildlife administrators to keep pace with the growing interest in the recreational use of raptors and the need to balance this interest against a growing level of orchestrated concern from protectionists were much more responsible.

The late Aldo Leopold, writing in *"A Sand Country Almanac"*, considered falconry to be "all in all the ideal hobby," a viewpoint many of the most intelligent men throughout recorded history share. While it has sometimes been a recreation of barbaric peoples, there is nothing barbaric about falconry. Archaic it may be, but no art with a classic literature in languages as diverse as Japanese, Korean, Chinese, Sanskrit, Hindustani, Persian, Arabic, Hungarian, Latin, Spanish, German, French and English, no art which has captured the imagination of some of the most brilliant men in every one of the diverse cultures these languages represent, can possibly be described as uncivilized.

For those who, ignoring the record of history, insist the classical, human recreational use of birds of prey causes them harm, an examination of the status of the saker falcon is most revealing.

The saker falcon is one of the largest falcons, second only to the gyrfalcon in size and strength. If not the direct progenitor of the gyrfalcon, it is certainly the species most like it in every way. Brown and Amadon in *Eagles, Hawks and Falcons of the World* list the range of this falcon as follows: "Central Europe and Asia from Bohemia and lower Austria east to Tibet and Manchuria. Migrant in winter south to Tunisia, Italy, Egypt, Ethiopia, Sudan, Arabia, North India and South China." Therefore, the combined breeding and winter range of this falcon exactly coincides with those geographical areas of the world which have supported a succession of the highest civilizations together with the greatest and the oldest densities of human population.

During this entire time (a period which spans at least three thousand years and encompasses all recorded human history), the saker falcon has been in continuous, unrestricted and un-interrupted commercial exploitation in areas where it could be easily captured during migration. It is still offered for sale on price lists from commercial trappers at prices averaging (in 1973) about $100.00 per bird.

If the commercial capture of a falconiform species for recreational use has any long-term, adverse effect for the bird, it should surely be indicated here.

What, then, are the effects of three thousand years of uncontrolled use and unrestricted commercial exploitation of a bird of prey? Of the saker falcon today, Brown and Amadon report as follows: "The saker is a bird of plains and steppes, high-level plateaus up to 11,000 feet (3,100 meters) . . . in steppes and plains it is the common large falcon. . . .In the breeding areas it can be very numerous, with pairs breeding only one or two kilometers apart; in such areas it tolerated a number of other species on the same crag with it . . . . It is a powerful, bold and aggressive bird, often used for falconry by the people of the middle east."

This statement is the historical verdict, the unequivocal judgement which time renders. If such unrestricted commercialization for human recreational use over so long a period has done this bird no harm, then surely the total statutory removal of North American birds of prey from all human use, as the protectionist organizations advocate, appears to be as fanatically ignorant as were the official wars of extermination.

Currently in North America raptors are administered and regulated as "wildlife," although what, exactly, is or is not "wildlife" has turned out to be more difficult to define than was the older definition of what constituted "game." Technically, wildlife administrators cannot regulate that which is not wildlife. Even in North America there are many animals and birds with populations both "wild" and "domestic," some of which defy classification in one or the other of the artificial categories. Moreover, the crossover is an ongoing process and continuously extends to encompass new species. Examples are so obvious and abundant as to scarcely require listing, but oysters, trout, frogs, rock-doves (pigeons), pheasants, ducks, geese, burros, goats and horses should do. The list could go on and on. If falcons belong on any list it is on this one —the list of animals so long utilized as to belong quite as much to man as to nature.

If some, not all, in the above list have any characteristic in common, it is that of having been altered slightly by the human selection of breeding stock. Those populations which have returned to the wild, therefore, have often retained some of the human-selected characteristics in some individuals. Claims to regulatory authority over these "feral" populations of formerly "domestic" animals are usually avoided by wildlife administrators, and in cases where such "wild" populations are protected, this protection is usually accomplished by special statute, separate and distinct from wildlife regulations. While historically the individual falcons acquired by humans have been derived directly from natural "wild" populations, yet historically too, all such capture, transport and use has been completely free of administrative control or interference; this being as true in North America as anywhere due to the "vermin" classification prior to 1970. Falcons have been administered as protected "wildlife" therefore for only a little more than a decade. In the same time period, however, a complete crossover from "wild" to "domestic" has been accomplished. The return crossover from "domestic" to "wild," also accomplished, has interesting implications because the population established is man-altered from a mix of North American and European wild stocks — a hybridization of subspecies as unlikely to occur in nature as is a beefalo — and the released birds are therefore more accurately described as "feral" than as "wild." If the human-altered, human-released city pigeons, on which these human-altered, human-

released city falcons feed, are not wildlife, neither are these falcons.

The technicalities relating to the regulation of sale and distribution of hybrid falcons, and even of falcons of such mixed sub-specific ancestry as above, are just as interesting. To qualify technically as wildlife for regulatory purposes, the life form must either occur naturally, or must formerly have so occurred in some natural habitat within the regional, federal or treaty-administrative area. If it does not, or never has, technically the regulators can make no claim to regulate. An example would be of bison, which occurred naturally in North America and are regulated as wildlife, whereas beefalo — the man-made hybrid of European ox and American bison — are a domestic farm animal to which wildlife administrators may make no administrative claim. Paralleling that, a domestic-bred peregrine falcon of any of the three North American subspecies is no different than those occurring in the wild and, accordingly, is still wildlife and subject to regulation as such. A hybrid falcon, and even some subspecies crosses, while obviously falcons, cannot be identified as occurring or ever having occurred naturally and are therefore, like the beefalo, man-made — a farm product, technically non-wildlife "domestic" and not subject to wildlife regulations.

The disruptive potential to regulations implied by hybrids, even by falcons of mixed sub-specific ancestry, is appalling to protectionists, wildlife administrators and enforcement personnel. Consider that virtually any combination of falcon hybrid can be produced through artificial insemination. Eggs produced by this method are not visibly different from other eggs produced by the same species of falcon. The fertile eggs may be incubated and the young reared entirely artificially, or incubated and reared by the falcon that produced them with or without the assistance of a male of the same or a different kind, or by a foster-parent or parents of the same species, or even by a foster-female or pair of totally unrelated species such as red-tail or Harris' hawk — or by any combination of the foregoing. In addition, hybrid young in the downy stages are not sight-identifiable. About one third of full-grown, first-year hybrids look sufficiently different — some strikingly so — to be obviously hybrids, but two thirds or more so closely resemble one of the parent species as to be still not sight-identifiable. Finally, these hybrids remain fertile even when they are hybridized with a third species. The resulting situation then is that only the breeder knows what kind of falcons he has and what kind of falcons have been produced, and this only if each egg is code-marked before hatching and each hatched chick further code-marked and recorded upon hatching. There is nowhere in the sequence where wildlife officials can effectively intervene to accurately separate pure species "wildlife" from the man-made farm product. Thus, from breeding or egg-producing adult to fertile egg and on to full-grown sub-adult, most falcons produced by private breeders are exactly whatever it may be to the breeder's advantage to record them as.

On legal ground so slippery and in a situation so unenforceable, court challenges or decisions are not in the best interest of regulators. Therefore private breeding and national-international sale — with appropriate permits — of privately produced progeny, preferably of identifiable species, seamless-banded, will be permitted. Legal, private ownership of seamless-banded falcons will be acknowledged. Gyrfalcons were "downlisted" in 1982 and allowed to cross international boundaries with appropriate permits issued by Canadian regional administrations. Arctic peregrine falcons were "downlisted" in 1984 to be made permit-available to American falconers during the autumn migration.

Unless a wildly improbable but possibly successful attempt is made immediately to artificially produce and officially record as an authentic natural occurrence, some hybrid falcons, thus establishing continuing regulatory control of all falcons as "wildlife" — the private ownership of raptors of domestic origin appears to have already escaped a too-tight regulatory straitjacket. Only the acquisition and ownership transfer of wild-caught raptors remains somewhat contentious, and this only because of the politically imposed "endangered" and "threatened" listings of falcons.

The rational administrative resolution lies in the application of a system that has been in practice for several hundred years and is continuously functional continent-wide. It lies merely in applying, to the capture of raptors, regulations parallel to those already in place relating to the hunting and acquiring of wildlife trophies. When a hunter "takes" (usually by shooting) any kind of trophy wildlife, the sale of the meat — as "game" — is prohibited, but the trophy of the hunt — anything from the antlers of a deer or caribou to the pelt of a bear, wolverine or wolf, or the skin and feathers of a grouse or duck — become private property. The transfer from public to private ownership is accomplished and acknowledged by the payment into public funds of whatever fees have been assessed for the permit, or for the permit and trophy-fee combined.

The same rules slightly modified to require live capture without injury, and legal retention as ownership-transferrable of only first-year birds, would allow the present trophy system to function perfectly for the private use of raptors. Certainly the successful hunt and capture, whether from the nest or later as a full-grown sub-adult, of a falcon or goshawk is quite as legitimate and high-quality an outdoor hunting experience as the hunting and killing of a bear or moose, while the quality and continuing value of the live trophy so acquired extends that experience indefinitely in new and exciting directions. There is nothing in the foregoing very bright or original. All this would have been an easy, established practice continent-wide by the mid-1970's had it not been for greedy, adversarial intervention during the mid-1960's.

Administrative trends of the late 1970's and early 1980's are pointing again in more rational directions. Probably from this point (1984) onward the somewhat artificial and oppressive interest in falcons and other raptors by non-falconers will wane. As these withdraw, lose interest and abandon formerly fixed positions, the trade in domestic raptors of all kinds and of both pure and mixed ancestry will become commonplace and essentially unregulated, while at the same time rational, regular, private-permit acquisition, transport, and trophy-fee ownership of falcons and other worthwhile raptors from the wild populations will again be restored.

Afield with a fine gyrfalcon ALICE KIMOFF

Falconry Equipment

The equipment required for falconry is both simple and inexpensive. The essential equipment is so basic and so easily handcrafted that the purchase of anything except the metal components is scarcely worthwhile.

Two leather straps, one on each leg, called jesses control raptorial birds. A swivel, or better a group of three swivels, attaches the jesses to a leather leash. The leash is then tied either to a leather glove the falconer wears on which the bird sits when being carried, or to a moveable block or a perch on the ground, or to a somewhat similar shelf or perch more permanently placed inside a building. In addition to the jesses, the bird also wears bells, one on each leg, which, like the jesses, it carries at all times. These bells serve the single purpose of permitting the falconer to locate his bird through sound. Many contemporary American falconers also attach a tiny radio transmitter trailing a short antennae to the tail of far-ranging species such as falcons. These transmitters permit the falconer to relocate birds which may wander many miles from their point of release. While such radio transmitters have prevented the permanent loss of many good birds, they are specialized and expensive equipment. The receivers must be carried in a vehicle and the birds may easily escape detection in areas where mountains, highlands or extensive marshes break up a continuous road-grid. Telemetry equipment has its greatest value and its greatest success in monotypic farming landscapes such as the prairies where an uninterrupted road-grid permits random cruising with the receiver operating. These monotypic farming landscapes also permit triangulation and fairly accurate spot-location of the position of the bird to within at least a mile of where it seems to be. Telemetry equipment is certainly not a guarantee against losing birds. While its use has resulted in the recovery of many good falcons, the sense of overconfidence resulting from its use has also been the direct cause of the loss of others. Telemetry equipment is a contemporary extension of the more primitive bells, but its use is not a substitute for inadequate training.

The hood is a device which fits over the head of the bird in such a way as to cut off all light without interfering with breathing or causing any other discomfort. The hood permits a bird to be carried without problems of fright. A hooded falcon can, for instance, be safely carried inside a motor vehicle at normal highway speeds, whereas an unhooded bird, no matter how tame, obviously cannot be carried under the same circumstances without risk of accident.

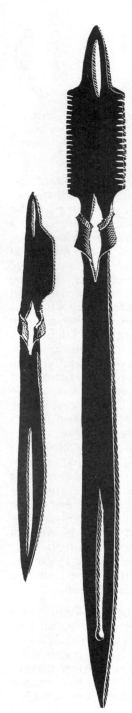

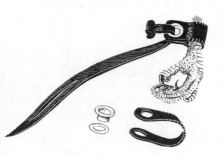

Aylmeri jess, showing method of attaching to the tarsi, gromet, and jess

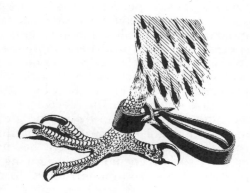

Traditional jesses, showing manner of attaching to the tarsi

Another item, the lure, is a tough, resilient effigy often made of leather in the form of a bird or a mammal. The lure is appropriate in relative size, texture and coloring to the kind of hawk or falcon being trained. A lure is the property and the prize of the falcon, but the falconer carries it out of sight of the falcon. The lure is the primary and the indispensable bond between falcon and falconer. Good lures and good luring techniques are traditionally perhaps the most-neglected aspect of falconry, considering their importance. The final item of equipment, which belongs entirely to the falconer, is simply a bag as elaborate, or as simple, as desired. Whether carried on a shoulder strap or attached to a belt, its function is to conceal and to carry the lure and any game which might be taken; or alternatively, during training, to conceal and to carry live quarries for release.

In review, a single bird requires this minimal equipment: two jesses, two bells, two bewits which attach the bells to the legs, three swivels, one leash, one hood, one perch, one glove, one lure and one shoulder or belt bag. Altogether, this equipment totals fifteen items, all of which, except the swivels and the bells, are easily and inexpensively handcrafted.

JESSES

Three types of jesses are used in contemporary falconry. These are illustrated together with an illustration which shows how they are attached. Oil-tanned "belly" leather, also known as "rawhide" (the same kind of leather used to make leather shoelaces) makes good jesses. However, the strongest and the most-enduring jesses are those made from kangaroo hide. The standard or the traditional jess is the kind most commonly used, except in the United States where almeryi jesses are currently mandatory. Almeryi jesses are made so the trailing part falls out if the bird is lost or otherwise away and free for any considerable period of time. This is its only advantage. Snap-on jesses are totally detachable and contemporary falconer-photographers have developed them as a method of photographing what then appear to be "wild" hawks in action. Except for this purpose, they are not good jesses to use.

Any bird being jessed for the first time must be held, and preferably hooded, in the hands of an assistant while the jesses (and bells) are being attached. Most trained birds can be outfitted with new jesses, new bells, or both without resorting to forceful handling if they are simply set on the gloved hand of an assistant while cutting off the old equipment and affixing the new.

BELLS

The making of good falcon bells requires skills in metallurgy which lie outside the interests of most falconers. However, excellent falcon bells are commercially available in North America.

Bells are made in various sizes to suit the relative sizes of hawks and of falcons. Three methods of attaching bells are illustrated. The kind of bewit shown is simple to make and it permits bells to be affixed while the bird sits hooded on the glove. Plastic electrician's "wire ties" also make good bewits for larger hawks and larger falcons.

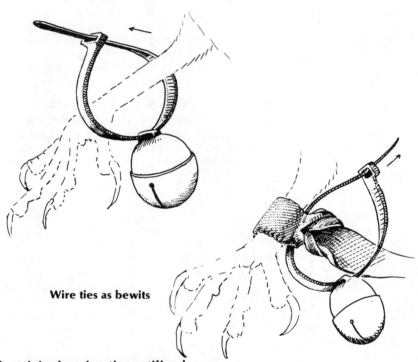

Wire ties as bewits

"Electrician's wire-ties utilized as falconers' bewits, showing two ways of attaching bells.

SWIVELS

"Sampo" ball-bearing swivels are available across the continent from sporting goods dealers. These swivels are manufactured in a wide range of sizes and they are tremendously strong, impervious to corrosion and exceptionally long-wearing. When utilized as illustrated in a group of three through the use of strong split-rings, a leash attachment results which never fouls and permits no twisting of either jesses or leash. This contemporary arrangement for the securing of trained raptors is much stronger, more reliable and more trouble-free than the single-swivel arrangement of traditional falconry.

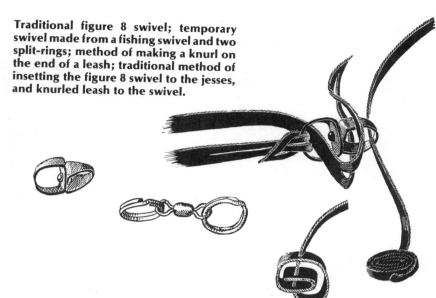

Traditional figure 8 swivel; temporary swivel made from a fishing swivel and two split-rings; method of making a knurl on the end of a leash; traditional method of insetting the figure 8 swivel to the jesses, and knurled leash to the swivel.

LEASH

The leash is so simple it requires little comment. Oil-tanned rawhide leather or latigo leather again make the best and the strongest leashes. Traditionally, the leash is tied to a perch or a glove, but knots in leather always cause wear and eventual weakening. The contemporary technique of slotting the jess at intervals permits the absolute securing of the leash without the use of knots.

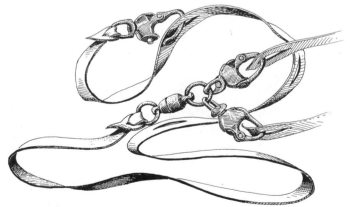

A leash arrangement for large strong raptors such as gyrfalcons, eagles or ferruginous hawks utilizing three swivel snap-shackles and a large sampo swivel. Brass snap-shackles of this type are available at ship chandleries.

HOODS

Beautifully hand-tooled, professionally-made hoods for birds of prey have become commercially available in recent years following a lapse of nearly two centuries. Nevertheless, the handcrafting of serviceable and well-fitting hoods is not a particularly highly-skilled procedure. A method of ascertaining the correct size of hood to fit a particular bird is illustrated here with the procedure necessary to complete a good hood. Hoods should be made of standard dry-tanned (not oil-tanned) leathers and common sense should indicate the thickness of leather selected; a hood for a small species should obviously be made of thinner leather than a hood for a large species.

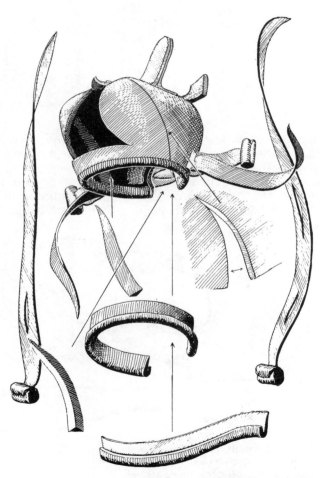

Seamless glued hood made from the Slijper "canon" showing parts and construction

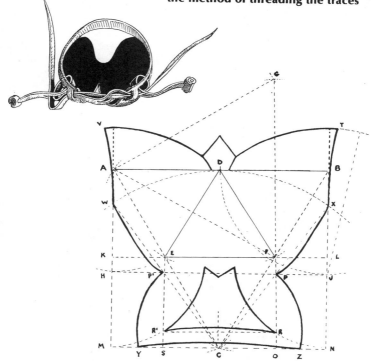

Falcon hood viewed from below to show the method of threading the traces

H.J. Slijper's "canon" — 1. A.D: Basic measurement of the head of the bird measured across the top of the head just behind the eyes; 2. A B twice A D; 3. A B C Equalateral triangle; 4. Line H J is located with centers at A and B respectively and radius A D and B D; 5. Points E and F are located with center at D and radius D A and D B; 6. D E F Basic equalateral triangle; 7. M N is drawn parallel to A B passing through point C; 8. A M and B N are drawn parallel to C D; 9. Project line E F to points K and L; 10. Point G is located with center at A and radius A F and with center at F and radius F A; 11. Line G O is drawn parallel to B N passing through point F. It locates two basic points on the hood pattern, P and R; 12. Line E S is drawn parallel to G O and locates points P1 and R1 respectively; 13. Outline D T; D V is located with centers at J and H respectively and radii J D: H D and are drawn out slightly beyond points A and B; 14. Points W and X are located with center at C and radius C D; 15. Outlines P Z and P1 Y are drawn to P and P1 respectively, locating points Y and Z; 16. Outline of the beak-hole is drawn with centers L and K respectively and radius L N and K M; 17. Y and Z are joined with a slight curve as shown, as are R1 and R; P X; P1 W; X T; W V to give the finished hood-pattern outline.

Hooding, as a daily practice in the training of a bird, requires a certain deftness of hand which must be learned. The first few hoodings of a newly-captured bird are somewhat arbitrary, but such treatment must not be continued for long. A hood with drawstrings is usually a necessity for newly-captured birds . The easily-removed, easily-replaced spring hoods are more suitable for birds which no longer object to being hooded and make no persistent attempts to remove the hood once it is in place.

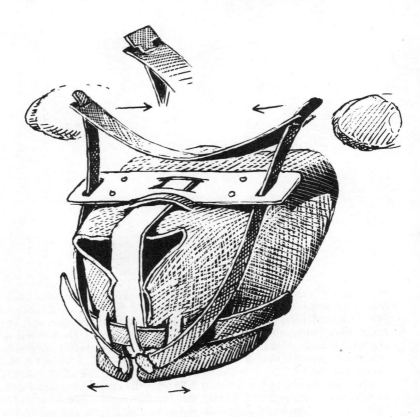

Compression-spring hood. The spring is a section of clockspring. The supporting structure illustrated is of 1/16" sheet metal but may be made of hardwood, horn or ivory. This type of hood permits quick precise unhooding of hawks in situations where the falconer is in control of stalking the quarry and timing the flush of such quarry. The hawk is unhooded just before the quarry is flushed.

Spring-closing hood

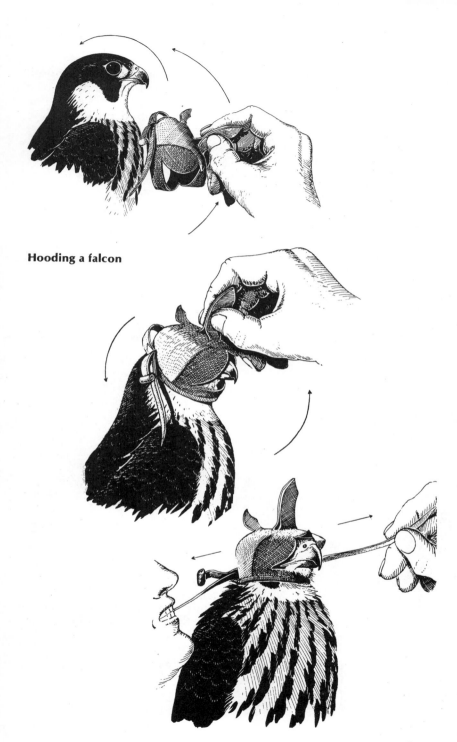

Hooding a falcon

LAWN BLOCKS AND PERCHES

Lawn blocks or lawn perches are devices to which a bird is tethered and which provide nothing more than a solid, raised perch or a surface for the bird to sit upon during periods when it is not being carried. Lawn perches are of two types: the tapered block being the type traditionally used for falcons while the "T" or the "D" perches are traditionally used for buteos, accipiters and eagles. Both types are built around a central metal pin pushed into the earth to hold them in place. Both types are illustrated.

Falcon blocks should be wide enough across the top to prevent any possibility of the jesses of the tethered bird encircling the top. The perching surface also requires texturing in order to prevent the development of foot problems. For this purpose, the artificial polyethylene grass, marketed under the name of Astroturf, has proven most satisfactory.

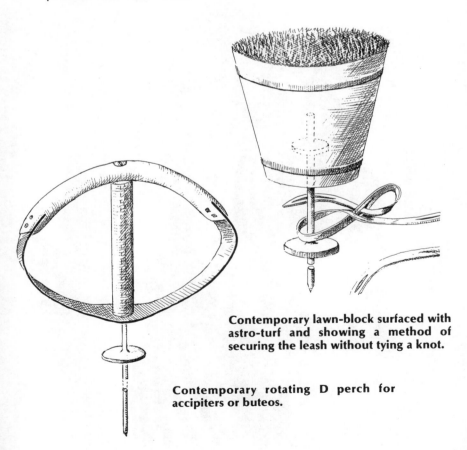

Contemporary lawn-block surfaced with astro-turf and showing a method of securing the leash without tying a knot.

Contemporary rotating D perch for accipiters or buteos.

The "T" or the "D" type hawk perches tend to foul the leash if they are constructed as a single solid unit. The rotating perch, which is illustrated, cannot foul the leash and is the most satisfactory type for accipiters and for buteos. Eagles are too large and too strong to be safely tethered to lawn perches, except when they are under constant surveillance.

Lawn blocks and perches are essentially for daytime, fair-weather use. Unless they are in a shaded area and surrounded with wire-mesh fencing, they should also be restricted to supervised use only. Some contemporary falconers are constructing tall perches for outdoor use. On these, the block or the perch is raised on the central support some four or five feet above ground-level. When such tall perches are used, or when a bird is similarly tethered to an inside-wall perch which is a similar distance above ground-level, the leash should not be secured at ground-level. Instead, the leash should be secured to a metal ring which can slide up the perch-support to just below the perch-level when the bird bates off. Ground-level tie-downs fling the bird violently to the ground and are a major initiating cause of foot injuries. The higher the perch is above the ground-level tie-down, the more pronounced and violent this result will be.

INTERIOR PERCHES

Interior perches, or perches arranged so the tethered bird can avail itself of shelter from wind or rain and at the same time be completely protected, are probably the most expensive, but the most necessary, requirements of falconry. Probably the easiest, but one of the best, ways to provide for the safety and the care of a hunting raptor is to keep it loose inside a small room or an outbuilding. A building or a room used for this purpose should be completely cleared of any stored materials or clutter. One or two shelf perches and perhaps a window-ledge perch should be provided; all these should be surfaced with Astroturf. Windows should be fitted with closely-spaced vertical metal rods or strong wooden dowels and an entrance compartment constructed which permits the closing of one of the entrance doors before the other one is opened. An equally-good alternative is to construct a roofless rectangular enclosure of plywood or of boards over which is placed tightly-drawn, strong nylon fish net or a metal mesh. On the inside two or three wall perches are again provided and surfaced with Astroturf, but a small, steeply sloping roof should be built over at least one of these perches. For human entry, the two-door system is always best.

Provision can easily be made in either of the foregoing for one or more permanently-placed blocks or rotating perches of the same type and the same height as the lawn perches. Such perches are most useful and most convenient as temporary, secure and fully-protected tie-downs for birds during periods when they are being frequently flown or frequently handled.

Raptorial birds have no absolute need for drinking water. However, some species and some individuals of most species enjoy bathing in shallow water at irregular intervals, especially during hot weather. The large plastic water containers manufactured for use as lawn-pools for small children make excellent baths for a falconer's birds. (Note: U.S. State and Federal regulations require that water be made available to the birds at all times.)

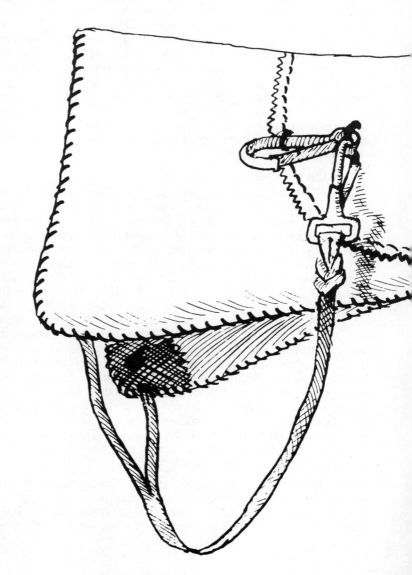

GLOVES

A right-handed falconer requires a glove for the left hand and the reverse applies if the falconer is left-handed. The smaller falcons and the smaller accipiters (the merlin, kestrel and sharp-shinned hawk) require only a wrist-length glove made of lightweight calfskin. The medium-sized to large hawks and falcons, from the Cooper's hawk up to and including the big ferruginous hawk, are better held on a gauntleted glove of considerably heavier leather,

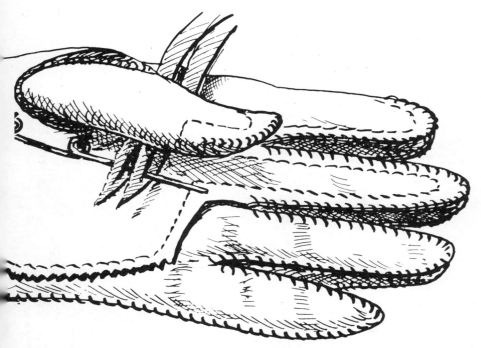

preferably one of double-thickness in the areas of the thumb and the forefinger where the talons tend to grip most frequently. Golden eagles, if they are handled on the glove at all, require a specially-made glove of heavy horsehide which extends upward nearly to the shoulder, but there are safer ways to carry eagles which do not involve carrying them on the hand. For most of the larger hawks and the larger falcons, welders's gloves adequately serve for carrying the birds. Certain small conveniences in the way of special fittings can easily be added. Some of these fittings and their uses are illustrated.

Falconer's glove equipped with some useful field attachments

LURES

In the training and the recovery of any falcon, except for only the little kestrel, a good lure is a necessity. It is also almost as important when working with any accipiters which are trained as bird-hawks. The lure required for these birds is an aerial lure which, to be effective, should as closely resemble a bird in appearance and in action as possible. For hawks primarily trained for flights to rabbits

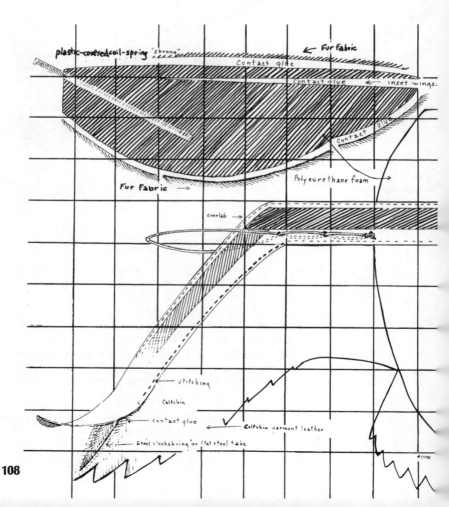

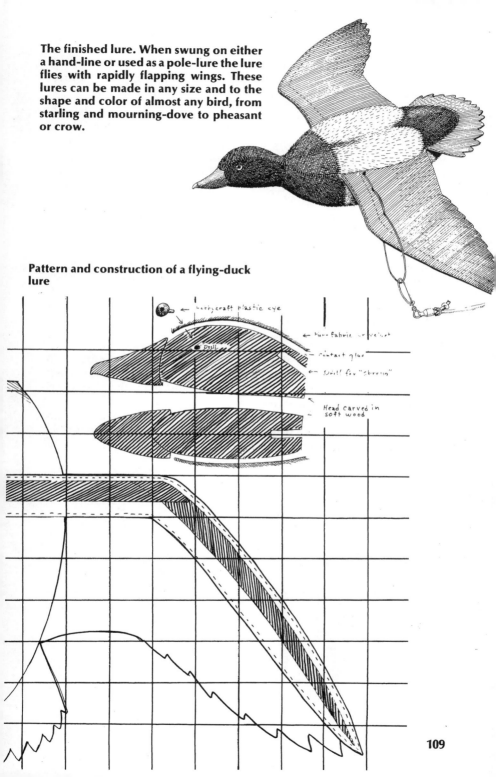

The finished lure. When swung on either a hand-line or used as a pole-lure the lure flies with rapidly flapping wings. These lures can be made in any size and to the shape and color of almost any bird, from starling and mourning-dove to pheasant or crow.

Pattern and construction of a flying-duck lure

furry-craft plastic eye

← fur-fabric or velvet

← contact glue

← Drill for "skreein"

Drill

Head carved in soft wood

or to hares, the use of a lure is optional. If used, it should be made to resemble a furred mammal and dragged along the ground rather than whirled in the air.

The type of falcon lure illustrated can be made in any size. In use as an effigy of any kind of quarry, it greatly resembles a live, flying bird. The metal insets at the leading edge of the calfskin-leather wings give it the "live" wing-action. These are cut from thin-gauge springsteel; clock spring is excellent for this purpose. The textured central body is made of two pieces of polyurethane foam covered with fur fabric — the "fun fur" of contemporary hobby shops. The head is shaped from wood and is covered in fur-fabric with a short, close nap. These lures can endure tough treatment and they can remain functional for years.

Ground lures are useful at times in the training and the recovery of rabbits and of hare hawks. These lures do not need wings and they are little more than resilient, fur-covered and elongated bags. Dyed and sheared sheepskin is an excellent exterior covering for these ground lures.

LURE BAGS

For the novice falconer, almost any kind of a bag or a pouch will suffice for a time. Most falconers eventually devise their own personalized design of a combined lure and game bag which is nearly always compartmented. One such compartment bag is illustrated, but as the size of the bag must also be relative to the kind of quarries or game most frequently carried, the type shown is only an example and it should not be considered a prototype.

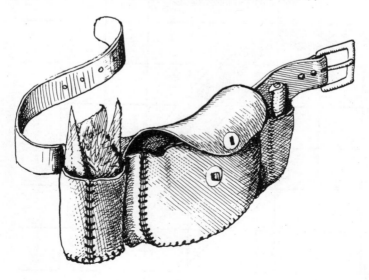

Capturing Wild Raptors

It has already been noted in the introductory chapters that the legal acquisition of hawks or falcons from the wild populations is currently in a state of political confusion and transition. While some people predict the time may arrive when the only birds allowed for falconers's use will come from breeders, it could be just as easily predicted, under modern conditions, falconry will not become sufficiently popular to support breeding as an economically-viable venture. Thus, within a relatively short time, falconry could revert to the historic situation with nearly all birds being taken from wild populations. More likely than either of these extremes is the development of a rational mix of both. Accordingly, a chapter on some of the ancient and some of the contemporary methods of capturing raptors is neither out of place nor outdated.

Raptors captured after they can fly are classified into four categories which relate to certain obvious age differences. "Branchers" are young birds captured near the nest during the first month to six weeks the parent birds still attend them. "Passage hawks" or "passagers" are also young when they are captured, but they are birds captured after they are fully independent, usually somewhere along the route of their first migration or "in passage." "Haggard" hawks are birds which are in complete adult plumage and, therefore, are at least three years of age, but probably much older. The term "first-year haggard" is a category between the passage and the haggard and it refers to a bird which has been through the first moult, but the bird still retains enough first-year feathers to indicate it is only two years of age.

The concept that fully-adult birds, when they are trapped, should at once be released is traditional in falconry. As most adults are breeding birds, it is a tradition based on common sense and falconers, especially experienced ones, seldom violate it.

Until the 1970s, the primary source of falconers's birds was the capture of first-year wild migrants, usually from professional trappers. As it is now known to be a biological necessity that ninety per cent or higher of this age group must perish during their first year, it is not surprising even large-scale removal of these birds from the wild populations has had no adverse effect on any species.

Through Europe and through Asia, the best places to intercept and to capture birds of prey have been known for centuries. Also in North America, there are many places where these birds tend to concentrate during migration. Slow-flying, soaring species tend to concentrate along ridges. Hawk Mountain, Pennsylvania, is probably the best-known example on this continent of this type of raptor flyway. A few accipiters, and even fewer falcons, also use this route, but ridges which concentrate buteos are not the best places for intercepting accipiters or falcons.

Water barriers, not hill ranges, are the geographical feature which most effectively concentrate bird-hawks because neither falcons nor accipiters tend to soar much when they are migrating. In North America, the best example of the type of shoreline which concentrates these species is found along the northwestern half of Lake Superior. From Duluth, at the westernmost point of the lake, the trend of the shoreline is uniformly northeast for a distance of about 120 miles (200 kilometers). Raptors moving south of southeast across a front of about 90 miles (150 kilometers) reach this shoreline and follow it, by veering southwest. These raptors increasingly become concentrated along the shoreline until they round the southwest end of the lake at Duluth, beyond which they again rapidly disperse. Enough goshawks pass along this shore annually to supply virtually every falconer this continent will ever know with a fresh passage bird every autumn while not affecting the number of breeding birds. The west side of north to south shorelines concentrates moving raptors in a similar way as do points oriented southwards or peninsulas along east and west shorelines.

In *North American Falconry and Hunting Hawks*, a number of specific places for capturing birds were listed; though less well known than Hawk Mountain or Duluth, falconers proved them to be good interception points. The result of identifying these places was immediate. Every place named was pre-empted and declared a sanctuary, each place was "protected" in some other way from falconers. One of the areas listed in the above-mentioned book as an excellent place to intercept migrating arctic peregrines was Assateague Island. This island is one of the lineal sand islands backed with dunes and saltmarshes which face the Atlantic Ocean. Such open reaches of sand and marsh which face open water tend to concentrate migrating falcons exactly the same way the western parts of Lake Superior concentrate goshawks.

In plains landscapes, raptors tend to follow large rivers or, more correctly, the rim of the hill-scarps which define the major river valleys. If one keeps in mind the fact raptors tend to move south or southeast with the northwest winds which follow the passage of a stormfront and, combine this fact with a study of detailed maps on a large scale, many places can be defined where passage hawks may be intercepted and may be captured without encountering interference.

Once the interception point along the route of migrating raptors has been reached, some of the trapping sets can be made semipermanent because, if it is correctly timed, a more or less constant flow of birds will pass. Failure to capture any particular bird is no great loss — another bird is almost sure to be along shortly.

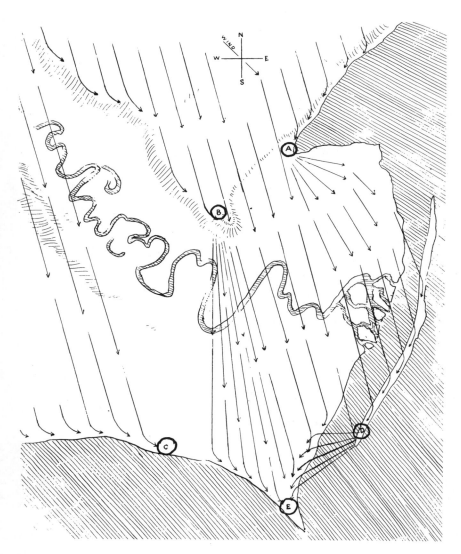

Diagram to show where land forms and shorelines concentrate migrating raptors. Accipiters and falcons will be found at A; buteos and some accipiters at B; falcons at D and all kinds at C and E.

Another way to find hawks suitable for falconry is to search for them individually on their winter ranges. Wintering raptors tend to occupy certain specific areas or "territories" for periods varying from days to months, depending on the food supply. The bird-hawks, the accipiters and the falcons are primarily attracted to congregations of other birds. Wherever these birds occur during winter, some kind of bird-hawk of a size relative to the prey is likely in the vicinity. Some of these wintering raptors are unconcerned and obvious while others are most unobtrusive and most secretive. In cases where peregrines, gyrfalcons or goshawks are wintering without human molestation in the vicinity of large populations of wintering waterfowl, they may be easily and frequently seen. However, should they be harassed or be persecuted or, if the bird community being utilized consists of a mixed congregation of species such as crows, gulls, magpies, ravens and starlings, they may be secretive as a means of evading harassment.

Some species which tend to winter on rather uniformly-distributed prey species are themselves somewhat randomly distributed. Species such as prairie falcons and ferruginous hawks, both of which are essentially non-migratory, are best located by cruising secondary roads at slow speed during late fall and winter while looking for them perched on utility poles, strawstacks or other elevated points. In addition to these, species goshawks, gyrfalcons, red-tails (of course) and occasionally even peregrines can be found this way and subsequently be captured.

Thus, the season for effective hawk trapping extends from about mid-August through to February or even into March; but throughout this same period, the first-year birds are themselves being eliminated. September and October trapping produces first-year birds in a ratio of some six or ten to every adult. Midwinter trapping (December and January) is less productive and produces first-year and adult birds about equally, but with the numbers of first-year birds decreasing rapidly thereafter.

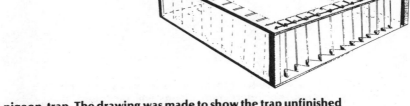

A pigeon-trap. The drawing was made to show the trap unfinished to emphasize the working mechanism more clearly. Bobbers may be put on one side only if so desired.

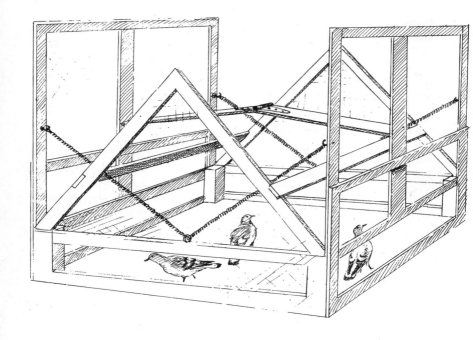

The Swedish goshawk trap showing details of construction

One type of effective, stationary trap is the Swedish goshawk trap. It is most effective when it is placed in an area where an initial lure in the form of free-flying game birds or pigeons are constantly present. This trap has been known to capture the occasional gyrfalcon, but generally it is ineffective for falcons. When the trap is sectionally built so it can easily be dismantled and quickly re-assembled, it is a most-effective trap for the capture of accipiters and buteos where they can be intercepted during migration.

All raptors appear capable of nearly-instantaneous discernment of the least flaw in the normal flight of other birds; even species which normally do not attempt to catch birds, nevertheless, immediately attack any bird smaller than themselves they can see is injured or is weakened. The more spirited bird-hawks are as discerning in this respect and even quicker to attack. Another universal characteristic is the tendency of larger species or individuals to pursue other hawks carrying food and attempt to snatch it from them. A third characteristic, particularly of falcons and of accipiters, is an abiding hatred of the large owls and a tendency to strike at them whenever they sense an opportunity to do so. Some of the more sophisticated and the more successful methods of capturing hawks and falcons take advantage of these tendencies.

From Arabia and from North Africa comes the trick of attaching a light feathered ball, festooned with nylon nooses (originally horsehair) to the jesses of a tame, but lightweight, slow-flying hawk, such as a Harrier hawk, which is carried about and released in sight of a falcon. The falcon always gives chase and seizes the noosed ball (known as a barak) which causes both birds to spin to the ground with the falcon usually secured to the barak-hawk with some of the nooses. Developed in the desert, this procedure is suitable only in open country free of trees, utility lines, water areas and deep ditches.

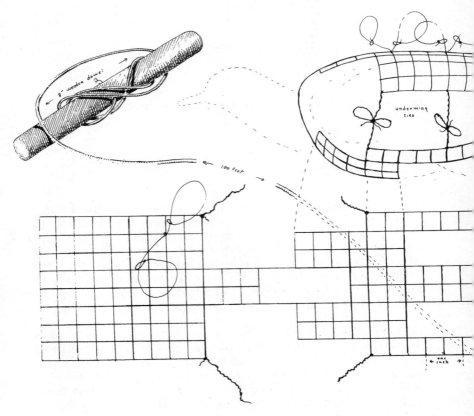

In a similar method, a pigeon can be fitted with a lightweight leather harness festooned with nylon nooses. The harness has a long line attached which is wrapped around and attached to a short wooden dowel. The pigeon and the wrapped line are thrown out of a vehicle as a perched raptor is passed. Although effective, this device captures only about half the hawks which attack and capture the pigeon. It is slightly more effective if the pigeon is hooded because it then makes no attempt to evade and is captured while most of the nooses are still open and are still functional.

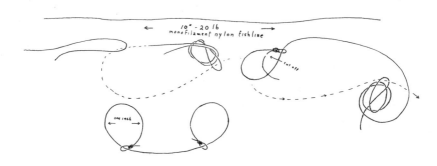

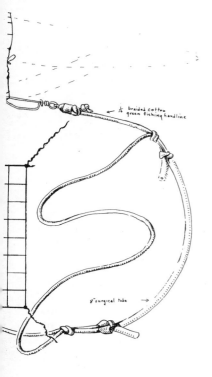

Method of tying double-nooses in nylon fishline for use on pigeon-harnesses or bal-chatri cages.

Mesh harness and run-out line for trapping falcons with a noose-carrying pigeon. The harness is made of ½" mesh herring net or fine ½ wire mesh. It carries ten to fifteen double-nooses tied to the upper surface only. Line wrapped about the dowell as illustrated will unwrap freely as the pigeon flies off without tangling.

Pigeons confined in a small Quonset or hemispherical wire cage festooned with nooses can be utilized in a similar manner, but because the pigeon is prevented from flying or even opening its wings, it is less likely discerned by the raptor. While less attractive to hawks than the harnessed pigeon, these traps (known as balchatri) are more effective in capturing those hawks which do come to them.

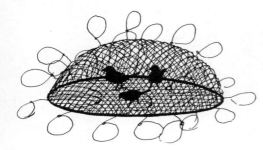

A bal-chatri trap. This style is excellent for the capture of small hawks.

Most hawks will return to a kill they have made themselves if they are driven off when feeding. Pigeons, unencumbered with the harness, but hooded and trailing the line and the dowel, fly higher and farther; as a result, they are more likely to be seen and to be captured than the harnessed pigeon. If the raptor feeding on such a pigeon is slowly approached and driven off, it usually will perch for a time only a short distance away. If a small rectangular net or a wire mesh festooned with nooses is then pegged down right over the dead pigeon, this noose-carpet is almost certain to capture the hawk on its return to the kill.

Pigeons attached to a line, which in turn is attached to the top of a pole in such a way a trapper hidden in a blind can lift the fluttering pigeon into the air again and again, are supremely effective in attracting hawks and falcons. Mist-nets, set at right angles to one another with the fluttering pigeon in the angle between, are effective in actually taking falcons. This same setup is, if possible, even more effective when a large perched owl is set between the nets. Accipiters are readily caught in the nets when the lure is an owl; if attacking the pigeon, accipiters tend to see and to avoid the net. A coarse, large net baited with a second pigeon and set so it can be activated from the blind will capture anything which comes in on either pigeon.

All the methods outlined here are equally effective in the capture of the smaller species, except for these, starlings are the appropriate bait species. Not only are they the right size, but they are also active, fluttery and, unlike most small birds, legal to use or to possess.

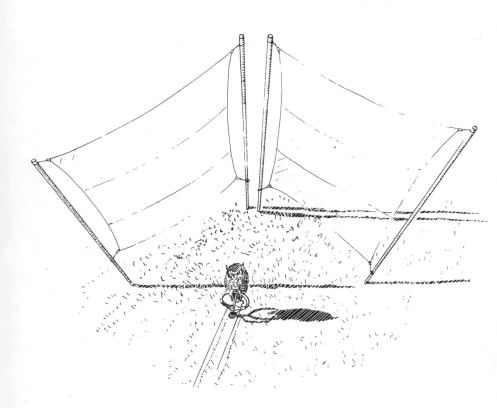

A mist-net for capturing falcons using a horned owl as a lure.

blind

← 75 to 100 yards →   Steel downrigger fishing lin

downrigger line

Contemporary trapping set for capturing hawks or falcons during migration. The line-up of blind to pole must always be at or nearly at right-angles to the wind-direction, with the net setting such as to throw the net downwind. The number of small lead-weights on the net-line must be adjusted relative to the size and weight of the net itself. Falcons that refuse to bind to one of the two pigeons and come to ground can be captured in flight by lofting the net downwind over them as they slow speed on an upwind strike-pass at the pigeon.

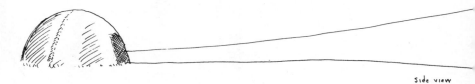

Side view

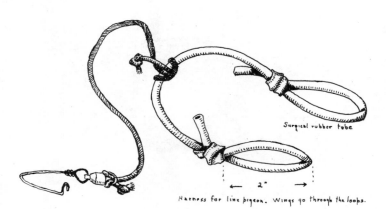

Surgical rubber tube

← 2" →

Harness for line pigeon. Wings go through the loops.

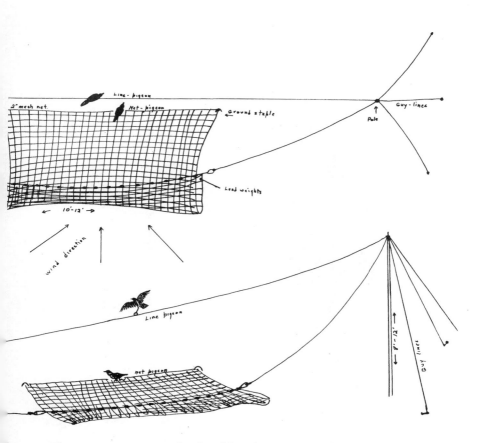

The more active methods of hawk trapping, those which involve the trapper and require continuous attention, are considerably more exciting than fishing and are, therefore, essentially recreational in their own right. Since the publication of *North American Falconry and Hunting Hawks*, in which most of these methods, some of them recent and some of them ancient, were described, bird banders and institutional researchers have "discovered" and to some extent pre-empted them. These men tend to consider the capture of raptors for their purposes somehow more legitimate and more acceptable than capture for falconry. In some areas, they have even succeeded in making the capture of hawks for falconry illegal. Without making any case here for the contemporary commercial capture of hawks for sale to falconers in the traditional way, it would seem the annual issue of regional-seasonal permits to allow the capture and the retention of a limited, but variable, number of first-year birds of specified species would be a rational way of achieving a dual recreational value for birds of this group. They do have, after all, the longest record of recreational use of any form of wildlife known to man.

Eyess versus Passager

The novice to falconry has better results with a young bird removed from the nest (an eyess) than with a bird captured later in the year (a passager). For his first hawk, the novice is advised to obtain an eyess. There are so many differences in behavior and in mannerism between the eyess and the passager that these differences require discussion. (Note: In the U.S. novices are not permitted to obtain and train an eyess bird, they must start with a passage red-tail or kestrel.)

The classic works on falconry, particularly those of English origin, extoll the virtues of the haggard falcon above all others. As noted before, contemporary falconers primarily avoid them because the haggards represent the breeding stock of the wild populations. They also have the reputation of being so easily lost they are hardly worth the time required to train them. It may be in former times, haggards were better understood, but today the eyesses are best known. In 1633, the falconer Latham wrote of the eyess: "But leaving to speak any more of these kinds of scratching hawkes that I did never love should come to neere my fingers, and return unto the courteous and faire conditioned Haggard Faulcon whose gallant disposition I know not how to praise or extoll so sufficiently as she deserves . . . ." Nevertheless, for the contemporary novice falconer, an eyess has all the advantages.

In strict reference to falcons, not to accipiters or other hawks, these advantages vary somewhat with individual birds. Generally, an eyess is a kind of inversion or mirror-image of the wild-caught bird with the faults of the one being the virtues of the other. The greatest single advantage of having an eyess is its tameness. When it is taken young, raised and fed by hand, an eyess has no fear of man. If an eyess is trained on or near the area over which it will later be flown, the bird will develop and attachment to that area and will become so oriented it will return to the area if it is lost anywhere within several miles of the area.

As Latham observed, the faults of an eyess are numerous. Eyesses are known for their bad habits. They scream for food and they are jealous and clutching in their feeding habits. They are slow to train and some must be trained just to stay in the air. Initially at least, they never have anything like the style and the confidence in hunting their natural quarries which appear at once in passage birds. Nevertheless, eyesses, if they are properly handled and if they are regularly flown, show a constant, slow improvement so by the end of their first season many learn the particular kind of hunting required of them. Once eyesses are fully trained, they may be as effective as wild-caught birds.

Some of the more irritating faults apparent in eyesses also tend to mend with time. Many screamers cease to make noise by their second season. Other faults, such as tree-sitting, also disappear as soon as the eyess begins to take quarry. The bird and the trainer slowly and often painfully must learn all of these things. It is slow going, but an eyess is not likely to be lost and there is time for it to learn.

It may be in classic times there was good reason to prefer the passager. Passagers are well mannered, quick to train and soon out in the field; but times have changed. Not that passagers behave any differently nowadays than they did then because they undoubtedly had the same tendency to leave suddenly to do their own hunting. However, in medieval Europe, the serf or the villein espying a falcon wearing bells was far more likely to attain favor with His Lordship if he gave such a bird a lure and took it up, or at least reported on its whereabouts, than if he shot an arrow through it. If the attitude relating to hawks continues to improve in North America to where it matches that in England in 1633, we may again fly passagers with equal confidence.

The great fault of the passager is the frequency of its loss and usually, unless the bird is equipped with a telemetry transmitter, the finality of such a loss. In every other respect, certainly on a first-season basis, they are superior to eyesses. Passage falcons never scream, they are easily hooded and they feed erect without jealousy and without mantling. In the air, they fly high and strong with great stamina and, of course, they know all about hunting. The longer either an eyess or a passager is kept, the more alike they become. An intermewed passager slowly loses some of its reserve and becomes like an old eyess. The eyess which has been hard-flown to quarry for two seasons or more takes on much of the character of the passager; becoming more reserved and showing much of the fire and the spirit of the wild-caught bird. It is the eyess which has been kept as a pet, sporadically flown or not at all and has never hunted or killed which will retain the juvenile mannerisms of the nestling. Such a bird will scream, clutch and mantle just as badly in its third year as it did in its first. This type of bird is Latham's "scratching kind of hawke" indeed, but it is the fault of the falconer, not of his falcon.

Passage falcons are often reluctant to attack birds such as crows and magpies which do not normally constitute prey species. The classic works on falconry abound with references and with instructions for overcoming this reluctance and for training the birds to attack large or otherwise difficult quarry. Here again the problem is the falconer cannot possibly know just what the prior experience of his passager with such species has been. With some passage birds, it is impossible to get them to tackle such quarry at all.

As clumsy and as inept as eyesses may be on early game flights when they are compared with passage birds, they do have this advantage: if they do not know what they can do, neither do they know what they cannot do and the falconer knows their full experience. The same situation which to a passage falcon is an instantly-recognized opportunity means nothing to an eyess. The only opportunity the eyess knows is the one the falconer sets up below it. As long as the trainer can, through timely interference, save an eyess from serious difficulties with large quarry, it does not find such quarry intimidating.

In summary, the eyess is best suited to the beginner and to those falconers who tend to become attached to an individual bird and like to keep it for a long time. It is also best suited to those falconers for whom replacement falcons do not easily come and who, therefore, prize the birds which do come to hand. The passage falcon is definitely for the experienced falconer, preferably one for whom the loss of a bird is not too seriously felt. For people who like falconry better than falcons and who like to trap and to train birds, the passager is ideal. The enthusiast for this kind of falconry can, with practice, have a bird flying in the field on game flights in only three to four weeks. Such a bird will show good sport for the remainder of the season or until it is lost. Once the season is over, the passager can be released. The falconer is not troubled with keeping a bird through the moult and he can forget about falconry until the next autumn. This action is traditional rather than contemporary falconry, but it can be good falconry indeed.

If passage falcons have certain virtues which can be favorably compared with those of eyesses, the same cannot be said of accipiters. With these hawks, the only possible reason for working passage or haggard birds is an eyess is not available. Bert and Latham, like many of the English writers, list the passage goshawk as the most-desirable falconry bird. However, it should be remembered goshawks have never been a resident breeding species in Britain and all British goshawks originated on the continent. In ancient and medieval days, the method of taming a newly-caught passage goshawk was most interesting and was undoubtedly effective, although a method scarcely adaptable to our century. Bert, among others, insists a new bird should be kept on the gloved fist for an absolute minimum of three days and nights which is a nearly impossible regimen to follow nowadays. When he adds the further necessity of constantly carrying the bird on the glove during the daytime for some weeks thereafter, such advice is discouraging to a modern falconer.

The extreme wildness, so much a part of most passage goshawks and other accipiters which the previous procedures are designed to break down still remains their greatest single disadvantage.

Goshawks are often still used in Germany where these birds are probably as well understood and as effectively flown by modern falconers as they have ever been. In modern Germany, almost without exception, it is now eyesses which are preferred. Not that passage goshawks are useless by any means, but they do have all of the shortcomings listed for the passage falcon and more. Briefly stated, the major problem in working the wild-caught accipiters is the extreme fearful wildness which is so characteristic of many individuals.

At any rate, with eyess accipiters, especially Cooper's hawks, most of these problems are not encountered. There is an occasional eyess which, like some passagers, refuses to tame; but for the most part, if they are properly handled and with some understanding of the nature of the accipitrine hawks, the eyesses become as quiet and as good-natured as most falcons. The best of them can almost become pets — except the tamer they are at home and toward their trainer, the more exciting and the more eager they are in the field.

Of the three large falcons, the most noticeable difference in behavior and in disposition between eyesses and passage birds occurs in prairie falcons with peregrines next and gyrfalcons least. In training gyrfalcons, it is often impossible to detect any difference between a passage bird and an eyess after as short a time lapse as three weeks. There is also little difference in behavior between eyesses and passagers in merlins and in kestrels, except for the fact eyesses of these species are usually extremely noisy birds.

The differences in individual behavior and in individual response of wild-caught accipiters is so great any comparison between species is difficult. In general, passage goshawks respond better than passage sharp-shinned hawks and sharp-shins respond better than Cooper's hawks. What is certain is far-northern goshawks are much more responsive and infinitely less concerned about being captured than are mid-latitude goshawks. Some wild-caught, northern goshawks are amongst the easiest of all hawks to train as they are remarkably like gyrfalcons in this respect.

The species which are primarily utilized for flights to ground quarries require less comment. Red-tailed hawks and Harris's hawks are remarkable for the comparatively insignificant differences between eyess and passager. One difference does persist, however, particularly with red-tails. As hunting hawks in the field, passage birds have a more pronounced tendency to soar. Conditions conducive to soaring cannot be controlled, but they can be avoided. To avoid loss, passage red-tailed hawks should simply not be flown during windy, blustery weather or on warm, sunny days between ten in the morning and four in the afternoon.

In the case of ferruginous hawks and golden eagles, which are much alike in disposition and in mannerism, the apparent tameness of eyesses is often unexpectedly and dangerously manifested in the form of aggressive behavior toward the trainer. Passage birds of these species are somewhat less of a hazard to train, a fact which the falconer must seriously consider in working with the eagle, if not as much with the hawk. Passage birds of both species have a tendency to soar, a characteristic especially evident in eagles.

Care and Attention

The acquisition of any kind of hawk or any kind of falcon carries with it much the same commitment to regular attention as does the ownership of any other kind of live animal; however, with the acquisition of a hawk or of a falcon, there is the added notation that the minimal requirements of raptors, especially during periods of inactivity, are rather less than those of more familiar domestic pets. With raptors, their lack of any real need for water to drink and the ability of all larger species to go without food for a day or two without any ill-effects permits considerably more casual off-season care than most domestic animals require. However, the proper care of raptors, if it is not difficult or if it is not demanding, is sufficiently specialized and sufficiently different from the norm as to require attention.

Unless they are taken during the first downy stage when they still require an external source of heat, the young of most raptors are perhaps the easiest of all young birds to raise to flying age. From the large downy stage until they attempt to make their first flights, young raptors have only four basic requirements. They need protection from physical violence, whether this violence be from cats, dogs, raccoons, owls or malicious humans. They must be protected from wind, rain and direct sun. They also need one full crop of meat each day. While they do not require much space, they need enough room to exercise their wings as these develop. Underfoot should be some fibrous rough-textured material into which they can dig their claws, but it must not slip or slide.

The kind of meat provided young hawks should differ between species. The more closely the meat provided resembles the normal variety adults of their species feed them in the wild, the better for the young bird. For young kestrels, for instance, grasshoppers or evicerated white mice are excellent foods. They will also thrive on starlings, pigeons or young chickens. With these and other small species, such as merlins and sharp-shinned hawks, the meat of birds up to the size of pigeons and smaller ducks is proper while meat from larger birds should be avoided. Any meat from large mammals should not be given at all. The large raptors, from the Cooper's hawk to the ferruginous hawk, can be given the meat of any of the larger birds, in addition to the flesh of mammals up to the size of large hares. An occasional feeding of beef or horsemeat will do no harm, but a steady diet of the meat of large mammals should be avoided. Only eagles can be continuously fed on beef or on horsemeat. Most breeders of raptors also breed coturnix quail as a continuous food supply for their raptors. Falconers can often obtain frozen coturnix from breeders on a continuing basis; coturnix quail is the best of all obtainable food.

As already noted, young raptors taken in the first downy stage require controlled warmth and frequent feeding of tiny pieces of meat completely free of bone and of feathers. Large downies of the small species require morning and evening feedings of small bits of meat, including some bone, feathers or fur. The larger species which need only one daily feeding as large downies and thereafter they also require some bone and feathers in their diet. Raptors swallow this rough material, much of which is indigestible, in varying amounts. This rough material is later ejected from the mouth as a kind of ovoid cocoon known as a pellet or a casting in which the bones are encased in the feathers and the fur. The casting of the pellet should be a daily occurrence with a properly-fed hawk and it can be a valuable indicator of the general health of the bird.

The excretions of raptors are known as mutes. The mutes are the combined excrement from the digestive tract and from the kidneys. The urates are pure white and, together with some clear, watery material, make up the bulk of the mutes. The fecal wastes are small, well-defined ovoid brown bodies; from the large hawks, these brown bodies are about one centimeter long. They are embedded in the white urates with which they are ejected. Often the first sign of ill health in raptors is indicated with a change, usually to green, in the colors of the urates, or with diffusion of the fecal material in the urates. All falcons drop the mutes straight down, although the young may attempt to defecate into space rather than on the nest-ledge. All other raptors, young and old alike, horizontally eject the mutes with considerable force. This manner of ejecting the excrement, in falconry jargon to "slice," is one of the most objectionable features associated with the keeping of accipiters, buteos and eagles. Falcons can be brought indoors with little danger of having them foul rugs or foul furniture if normal precautions are taken, but other raptors can certainly prove embarrassing.

Shortly after the tips of the first plumage begin to break out of the feather sheaths, hand feeding should cease. The young birds can be given their daily food in large pieces and they can be permitted to tear it for themselves. This type of feeding should be continued until they are almost ready to fly.

With eyesses, some of the early procedures of training can be integrated with the growing experience. To this end, bells and jesses can be affixed to the tarsi a week or more before the young bird attempts to fly. During this same pre-flying period, tying the daily ration to the lure so the young bird feeds from it is an easy way to begin the association of the lure with feeding. A young bird can even be encouraged to chase and to capture the lure on foot well before it can fly. With eyesses, the first flights, however short, can also be to the lure. These can be increased each day until the bird is full-fledged and flying well. During the latter part of this same period, the bird learns to perch on the gloved hand of the trainer in order to be carried about. The bird can also learn to accept the hood as the somewhat unpleasant, but the regular, preliminary to a pursuit and capture of the lure, with a meal to follow.

By the time an eyess reaches the age at which most passage hawks are captured, it can be so advanced in its training that subsequent loss is unlikely. Some will even have had their initial flights to live quarry, but no eyess at this age can possibly have attained the experience and the skill in the actual capture of live quarry which any passage hawk of similar species and of similar age has attained. Moreover, because every passage bird has learned it must kill to eat, its pursuit of quarry is highly motivated. This motivation is not always the case with eyesses, which, of course, have learned just the opposite — failure to kill does not result in continued hunger.

Nevertheless, from the moment of its capture onward, the experience of a passage bird taken for falconry is convergent with the experience of an eyess. One does not fly the more spirited raptors for long before realizing whatever it is which motivates these birds in pursuit of their prey transcends hunger. The evolutionary reason for this characteristic is obvious. If the males were not highly motivated to pursue and to kill far in excess of their own needs, the females would not lay eggs, nor would the tiny young be fed. If both sexes were not similarly motivated later, their growing young would starve.

In raptors, this evolutionary drive is not confined to the breeding season or to the birds of reproductive age. Therefore, this evolutionary drive is why eyesses are eager to hunt and to kill regardless of whether they are being well fed or not. It is also why passage birds, even when they are relieved of any necessity of killing to eat, also remain eager to hunt. It is this fundamental fact which makes falconry possible.

PASSAGERS

The integration of early training with the daily care of eyesses is the only reason anything pertaining to training has been mentioned in this chapter. The daily care of passage birds is not closely linked to their initial training. This fact means any passage hawk which the falconer has trained, flown to quarry and repeatedly recovered and retained until the shortest days of the year has largely completed a convergent experience which makes it, from then on, little different than an eyess.

Much more than eyesses, wild-caught hawks tend to break their feathers. Also, some individuals tend to break their feathers while others do not. In addition, there is a marked difference in species; buteos and eagles seldom damage their plumage at all while wild-caught falcons are only subject to occasional damage. Passage accipiters of all kinds and Cooper's hawks nearly always damage some feathers.

When the long feathers of the wings or the tail are only bent, twisted or have the webs in disarray, they can easily be straightened if the bird is securely held and hot water is directly poured onto the feathers. This practice will immediately straighten the feathers. Broken feathers should be sheared off at the point of the break; great care should be taken not to crush and so split the shaft. Sharp side-cutters are the best tool for this removal.

The technique of rejoining broken feathers, a procedure known to falconers as imping, is illustrated. Imping broken feathers should not be casually undertaken because it usually involves forcible handling. Accipiters resent this handling and if it is associated with the falconer, he will remain unforgiven for weeks. Except with very tame hawks, imping should be undertaken only when the bird requires the use of the broken feathers. Any birds which are being regularly flown free to quarries should certainly have any broken feathers mended at once, but any birds still involved in training, or birds which have begun or are near to the moult, are just as well left alone.

When imping is necessary, especially when a wild-caught accipiter is involved, the bird should be handled in such a way so it makes no visual association between its trainer and this unpleasant experience.

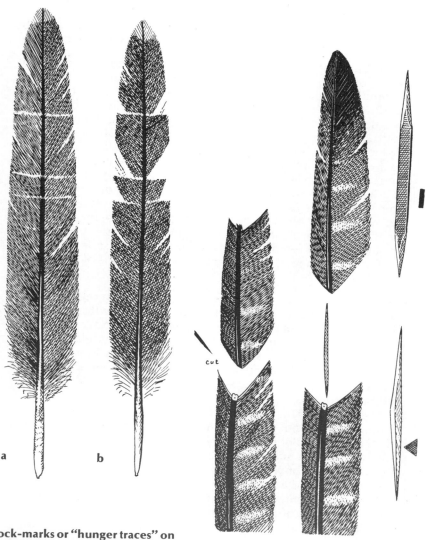

Shock-marks or "hunger traces" on the dark feathers of a peregrine to show the appearance of (a) a new feather showing such marks, and (b) an old feather damaged by shock-marks.

cut

Steps in the splicing, or "imping" of a peregrine primary feather to show how damaged feathers can be repaired, and showing two types of imping needles.

a

b

As already indicated, one answer to the problem of summer care with passage hawks is simply to cut off the bells and the jesses and let the birds go. This procedure has a long and an honorable tradition in Asia, but in North America there is still the real possibility tame hawks may be shot. Eyesses should never be released because they are almost certain to be destroyed.

The keeping of a bird of prey throughout its second summer and hence through the first moult is known to falconers as inter-mewing, the term "mews" being the old English word for the building in which hawks were kept. Traditionally, all birds were "put up," that is they were not flown at all during the moult. This moult should begin in April and be completed near the latter part of September, but all too frequently it is not. The internal biochemistry which controls moulting is not well understood. It appears to be delicate and it is somehow linked to feelings of security and of well-being. The often remarkable difference in the timing and the regularity of the moult between eyesses and first-year wild-caught birds of the same species indicate these feelings. The tradition of isolating birds in the mews during the spring and the summer and feeding them well, but otherwise leaving them rather strictly alone, is surely a result of generations of experience with difficulties in the moulting of passage birds.

Eyesses usually moult with such precision and such regularity they may be flown throughout the moulting period with no ill effect other than extending it two or three weeks. Passage birds kept active into the spring may have the onset of moult delayed one to several months. A bird which begins to moult in June or in July cannot possibly be finished until October, November or even later. Progesterone, the active ingredient in birth control pills, has been used with some success in initiating the accelerating moult in passage raptors. This ingredient is administered in doses of ten milligrams daily until moulting begins, at which time the dosage is reduced to five milligrams. Thyroid extract has also been used, but probably all such substances can have undesirable side-effects, whether they are obvious or not. Warmth, daily repletion feeding, plenty of light and a situation free of stress is probably the safest combination to initiate and to maintain a rapid, clean moult in wild-caught birds of prey. The placing of the bird by February or March in a moderately-sized, heated and well-lit room or building in which it is free to move about at will is the most practical contribution towards the objectives. One constant association should be maintained: the regular arrival of the falconer with food. If the bird is permitted to eat about half of each meal from the lure with the falconer present, then gently picked up with the lure and the other half eaten with the lure held in the gloved fist, the return of the bird to active hunting for its second season can be smoothly and easily accomplished.

The loss of one of the large primary feathers first indicates the onset of moult. Falcons usually first lose the seventh feather from the outside while all other raptors first lose the tenth. The moult is completed with the loss of the outermost primary feather in both groups. During the time interval, most of the remaining plumage is in process of being simultaneously shed and regrown. Many eyess falcons succeed in making a complete and perfect moult; in so doing, they undergo a profound change in appearance. Eyess buteos also frequently moult clean. Passage birds of any kind seldom shed all their first-year plumage during the first moult, nor, as a rule, do eyess accipiters while passage accipiters never do.

The rather scruffy, patchy-plumaged birds which result are not abnormal because the same incomplete moults are found in wild hawks and wild falcons. The knowledge incomplete moulting of first-year birds is neither unusual nor unnatural is of considerable

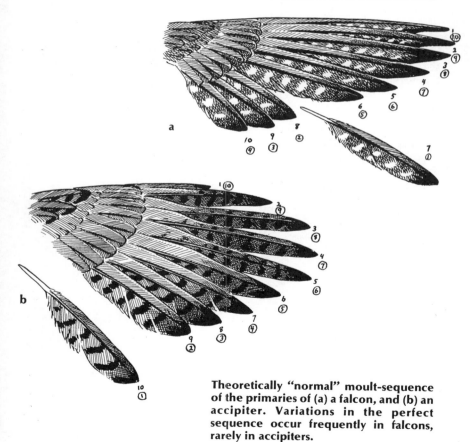

Theoretically "normal" moult-sequence of the primaries of (a) a falcon, and (b) an accipiter. Variations in the perfect sequence occur frequently in falcons, rarely in accipiters.

135

importance to a novice falconer. This knowledge permits the falconer to ignore the perfectionist myth in certain literature of falconry which holds a second-year bird should not be leashed and be brought out of the mews until it has completed the first moult.

As a rule, these worn and tattered remnants of the first-year plumage are the first feathers to be shed with the onset of the second moult, but there is the occasional accipiter or eagle which will retain one or two first-year feathers into its third year of life. The large wing and large tail feathers should be collected as they moult out and they should be stored as a feather-bank for the replacement of broken feathers.

Birds taken up from the moult should be critically examined. Some birds will have developed overgrown beaks, overgrown talons, or both which should be cut back. Beaks are best coped with side-cutters. This coping, as well as any coping of the claws, can usually be accomplished with the bird merely hooded and placed on the glove of an assistant. Coping the talons with side-cutters results in blunted claws, but this blunting is not important if the bird is not soon to be flown to game. Otherwise, the better way is to pare the claws back along the inside curve of the talon with the knife-edge of a narrow-bladed knife. This method results in shorter but sharper claws.

At the same time, the feet should be carefully examined on the underside for any signs of corns or of swellings. Particular attention should be paid to the center pad at the base of the toes and the rounded ball at the base of each talon. These areas are where foot problems nearly always originate, especially with falcons.

These problems concerning the health of the bird can have serious consequences if they are not promptly and correctly treated on discovery.

Training

The evolutionary limitations of a particular species equally limits every falconer, no matter how experienced or how skilled, in any attempts to train a particular bird of prey. Some golden eagles can be trained to attack and to kill wolves, but it is obviously foolish for any falconer to think he can somehow train a red-tailed hawk to accomplish the same task. Although less obvious, it is equally absurd to imagine a red-tail can be trained to hold a position high above the falconer and to stoop to winged quarries as does a peregrine. While they are highly aerial, and under certain wind and weather conditions can rise to commanding heights, red-tailed hawks are no more falcons in spirit or in disposition than they are golden eagles in dimension and in strength. A red-tail will do only what it can do. Evolution governs the performance of the red-tail, not the dreams or the expectations of its trainer.

To be successful, the training of any kind of raptor must be oriented toward encouraging the best field performance of which the species is capable, but some species are not capable of much. The simplest and the least spectacular flight of a trained hawk is essentially no different from that of a mouse-buzzard which flies from a perch on a post to capture a mouse or a grasshopper on the ground. The only difference is the trained bird leaves a perch which happens to be the gloved hand of its trainer. Also, just as the wild raptor, whether it catches the mouse or not, will often return to the same perch, the trained raptor is specifically conditioned to return to its special perch. It is this returning, far more than the outward flight to quarry, which is the essence of its training.

Even the most advanced flights with large falcons are merely adaptations of the normal behavior of these same species in the wild. The classic "great flight" of the female gyrfalcon to a kite or a crane essentially is the same as the action of the female gyrfalcon when she goes aloft to assault an eagle trespassing in her breeding territory. Even the act of faith the "noble" peregrine exemplifies as it "waits on" in expectation of flushed quarry high above her trainer is not significantly different from the behavior of a wild peregrine which has similarly placed itself high in the air above some particular place where previous experience has indicated quarry will usually appear.

Between these extremes lie all the other flights of trained raptors with an infinity of variations. However, the only significant differences between the trained and the wild raptor of the same species and sex are these: the willingness of the trained raptor to ignore the presence of the falconer if it has captured prey, the willingness of the trained raptor to return either directly to the falconer or to his lure if it has failed to capture prey and, in some cases, the willingness of the trained raptor to permit the falconer or his dogs to be of service to it in the flushing or the routing out of potential prey.

Rough-legged hawk, adult in light phase.

- Frank L. Beebe

Each of the species which has evolved a more advanced way of capturing increasingly active or increasingly aerial prey never entirely abandons the ways of less highly-developed species. Thus, a gyrfalcon, wild or trained, may at times see and fly down to capture a lemming, a mouse or a shrew in a manner no more spectacular or no more exciting than the flight of a rough-legged or a broad-winged hawk to the same kind of quarry. However, needless to say, no rough-leg or no broad-wing will ever cut down in headlong flight a mallard or a pheasant in the grand manner of a gyrfalcon.

Humans have never been fascinated or enthralled with raptors such as rough-legs or broad-wings which fly only to tiny, slow-moving quarries. The species which arouse the attention of man are those which attack quarries so large or so swift the outcome has the potential of a contest of speed, strength or courage. It is at this point, concerning only those species which have the capability of undertaking the pursuit of active, alert, medium-sized or large ground quarries, the training of hawks begins.

In North America, the four species always capable of these flights are the red-tailed hawk, ferruginous hawk, Harris's hawk and golden eagle.

The evolutionary position of these species is about midway between a commitment to energy conservation and a more dynamic way of life based on a higher utilization of energy. In the training of any of these raptors, this ambivalence is often their most annoying trait. Usually, these are amongst the easiest birds of prey to train to come to the glove or to the lure, but they are often rather difficult to persuade to exert themselves in the pursuit of game.

FIRST FEEDING

Every passage raptor trapped for the purpose of falconry should be given the opportunity to feed from the gloved hand of its trainer as soon as possible following capture. Quite often, newly-caught first-year birds are ravenously hungry and will eagerly feed, especially if they are taken into dim light. Instead, if they are permitted to feed in isolation, a most important opportunity is missed. Birds which have been allowed this initial independence and have been permitted to eat their fill a few times may require this practice to continue, but on sharply-reduced rations and with the falconer always present when the food is offered, insistently coming closer to the bird as it feeds each day. The time soon comes when the bird can be picked up on the glove if the trainer takes hold of the meat with the gloved hand and lifts both together. The time required to accomplish unconcerned feeding from the glove and suspicion-free carrying on the glove will vary with different individuals and different species from only two or three days to as long as two weeks. Red-tailed and Harris's hawks are usually more responsive than ferruginous hawks and golden eagles in this phase of training.

CREANCE

The next step, whether with eyesses or passage birds, is to persuade them to fly increasing distances to the gloved hand for food. However, at this point, eagles are much safer if they are carried on, and flown to, a "T" perch held with both hands a little above the head of the trainer. Eyesses of any of the three species of hawks can be flown completely free during this phase of training, but passage hawks and all eagles, whether they are eyesses or passage birds, should be flown on "creance." The falconer's creance is merely a strong line which prevents the bird from flying away. The arrangement which gives the best control and prevents the bird from going up to utility poles or over utility lines is a smooth ground line forty to fifty yards long stretched taut between two posts or two pins. The jesses of the bird are secured to a much shorter line of two to three yards long which, in turn, is attached to a ring encircling the ground line. The bird is then placed either on a low post or transferred to the gloved hand of an assistant. The trainer walks a few paces away straight along the ground line and places a small bit of meat on his glove (or on a clip or a pin on the "T" perch). If the distance is short enough and the bird is sufficiently hungry, the action results in a first flight which is accordingly rewarded. This procedure is immediately repeated four or five times in quick succession with the distance of each flight increased one or two yards, after which the bird is permitted to finish the ration while on the gloved hand as the falconer slowly moves about as it feeds.

The same procedure must then be followed at the same time of day every day for a period which varies with the individual and the species from four or five days to as long as two weeks. The distance of the flights is steadily increased until the bird is flying upwards of seventy-five yards or more. The time set for this exercise can be either early in the morning, just before or just after sunrise, or in the evening right after sunset. A whistle or reed-call can be used, or the bird can be silently worked by sight only. Developing an association to sound has some merit, particularly with Harris's hawks, but it is less important with the other essentially open-country birds than with the next group.

To ensure a quick, definitive response, these hawks should be sparingly fed during this next phase of training. The daily food intake should only be about fifty grams and not more than 100 grams even for an eagle. Their ability to conserve energy is really remarkable. Usually, only a real hunger will make them quickly respond.

The next stage of training can start after any of these birds will unhesitatingly come to the glove or "T" perch three or four times in succession for distances of thirty-five to fifty yards for Harris's hawks and red-tails and double that distance for ferruginous hawks and eagles. When they learn to sit on the glove in an unsuspicious and an unconcerned way and permit themselves to be carried about before and after feeding without frequent "bating" (the falconers's term for trying to fly), they are ready for the second phase.

ENTERING

At this point of training, many falconers "enter" these hawks to free-flights at quarry and terminate their formal training at this stage; indeed, many passage birds and a few eyesses will be capable of good field performance immediately after they have been successfully "entered." Entering is a procedure again based on a nearly universal characteristic of birds of prey. When a raptor migrates or otherwise moves for any significant distance, it often finds itself in an area where the prey species it formerly utilized does not occur. Under this condition, hunger soon presses the raptor to make attempts to capture any one of a wide range of unfamiliar quarries, most of which escape, until it eventually makes a kill. The kind of animal or bird which is captured and the conditions surrounding its capture are remembered. The next try for quarry will as closely duplicate the first success as possible. If this try is also successful, and the kind of new quarry, now twice taken, is reasonably abundant, the hawk increasingly takes a "set" to this kind of prey as long as it remains in that particular area.

In a British review of one of the earlier falconry books, it was pointed out some of the procedures outlined in the paragraphs which follow are illegal in Britain. As this present book is being prepared primarily for American and for Canadian readers, these procedures shall be included, but with this added caution. The use of living and somewhat handicapped quarries for "entering" hawks and falcons is the kind of thing politicians and lawmakers now call "socially sensitive." It is certainly one of the aspects of falconry which, if not done discreetly, can direct criticism and hostility toward falconers. Entering is usually not a requirement in the training of wild-caught raptors and it will, as the skillful use of lifelike lures becomes better known, altogether eliminate any need for living handicapped quarries.

There are four requisites to successful entering. The first is the bird about to be entered must be more than ordinarily hungry; the second is the quarry to which it is about to be entered must be, if not exactly the kind of quarry the falconer has in mind, at least something which resembles it in size, color and action; the third is the quarry be caught, killed, and eaten. Finally, and most importantly, the entire experience must be repeated two or three times in unbroken sequence under circumstances similar to the field conditions for which the bird is being prepared.

As most of the birds in the group presently under discussion reach their highest potential as rabbit or hare hawks, the acquisition of suitable entering quarry is not difficult; domestic rabbits will do. However, if cottontails are to be the quarry, small brown rabbits should be selected, but if winter flights at snowshoe hares are the objective, medium-sized white rabbits are more appropriate.

The best way to prepare the raptor for entering is to place it in isolation, preferably in darkness, for a period of 48 hours from the time of the last feeding period. If the bird is one which has been regularly hooded, it should be hooded in the dark and be brought to the area where it is to be entered. Otherwise, it should be transported by picking it up and carrying it on the glove in the way and at the time to which it has become accustomed.

If the assistant is to release the rabbit, both should be hidden. If the falconer is alone, the release should be made with the use of a trip-cord or an electronic spring-box which releases the rabbit and abruptly bounces it out, causing it to run. The area of release can have well-separated bushes or grass tussocks, but it should be completely devoid of any dense bush refuge or holes in the ground. If a wild rabbit or a hare is used, it should be handicapped or even tied so it can run just so far before being halted. The whole purpose of entering is to give the bird the conviction this particular kind of quarry, when seen, can be caught and be eaten.

It will be found, however, not all birds can be entered at this stage of training. While entering at this stage has few drawbacks for Harris's hawks and red-tails, it can result in later problems in field recovery with the more wide-ranging ferruginous hawks and golden eagles.

TO THE LURE

The ground-lure, merely a kind of furry effigy of a rabbit, has been described. Eagles being prepared to fly foxes should be provided with a fox-skin lure of appropriate size. The initial training to the lure should be merely a variation of the flight to the glove with the bird still secured to the ring on the ground line. The first flight to the lure can be with the lure held in the gloved hand (or secured to the "T" perch), but, in this case, with a significant chunk of tough, stringy meat, or a carcass held together with bone and sinew securely tied to the lure. The moment the bird begins to feed from this meat on the glove, the lure and the attached meat are forcibly jerked away from the bird and dropped to the ground. Most birds will immediately follow it down and resume feeding on the ground. Most birds also undergo an instant change in manner and demeanor toward their trainer at this point. With the trainer no longer at their level, but towering above them, they usually "mantle," spreading their wings and their tail over the lure and turning to face away from the falconer.

The falconer must now bend down, secure the lure in the gloved hand and lift the bird and the lure back up to the standing position. This action can be an awkward moment, particularly with eagles, and caution is recommended because the reaction of any individual bird is not predictable. Initially, all birds interpret this action as an attempt to steal their food; as a result, some birds aggressively react. Once the standing position has been resumed, the lure is again abruptly jerked away. This time it is tossed outward from the falconer for a distance of three or four yards with the bird free again to follow it down. This action can be repeated once more, but at the conclusion of the third flight from glove to lure the bird should be permitted to feed from the lure with the falconer standing or moving nearby until about half the food on the lure is consumed. Then lure and bird are again picked up together and the feeding completed in the usual position.

At the next session the following day, the bird can be held on the glove. The lure, with the meat attached, is produced and tossed out for a distance of five or six yards. When picked up this time, the lure, instead of being thrown out again, is taken away and immediately hidden. The bird is then transferred to a post or to the glove of an assistant and the falconer quickly moves some fifteen yards back along the ground line and either tosses the lure out, or better, produces the lure attached to a three or four yard line and drags it along the ground away from the bird.

As soon as the raptor regularly takes the lure in motion, free-flights from the falconer to the lure should be initiated. From then on, every improvisation and every variation which can be devised should be introduced. By using fairly long lines to drag the lure and by running the line around a pin set in the ground so the assistant, or even the falconer himself, can run at right angles or in the direction opposite to the moving lure, any fixed association of the lure with the position of the assistant is cancelled. Nevertheless, while it is desirable to have the bird eager to pursue the lure whenever it appears, one should always remember the real purpose of lure-training is to ensure long-distance flights back to the falconer under field conditions. For this reason, it is well to maintain some association with the two. When a ferruginous hawk or a golden eagle either goes to or comes to the lure for distances approaching a half-mile, it is really ready for entering and, immediately following, for flights to wild quarries.

Accipiters

Now to the accipiters which are more exciting and more rewarding once they are trained and they are in the field. As already noted, the largest of the group, the goshawk was more valued historically and, to some extent, currently than any falcon as a hunting bird over much of Asia. Mostly because northern Europe has no indigenous large buteos comparable to the North American red-tailed hawk and the ferruginous hawk, female goshawks in Europe have a background of being primarily trained to rabbits and to hares. While female goshawks, particularly the large European birds, are indeed competent at such quarry, the flight does not bring out the full potential of this species. As the Asian experience indicates, they are capable of much more.

The accipiters are dedicated bird-hawks and, if given the chance, they will take an extremely wide variety of winged quarry. However, they do not fly great distances in active pursuit, like falcons, and they do not deliberately seek the advantage of height. Their successes depend on surprise and rapid acceleration, a combination which, at its best, makes a superb combination of man and bird.

As forest birds which occupy an environment where vision is often restricted, the accipiters have become almost as oriented to sound as they are to sight as a means of locating their prey. They learn to recognize the calls many of their prey species make and they will move toward such sounds when hunting. Unlike the buteos and the eagles, which usually prominently perch in the open and are easily seen, the accipiters tend to perch low, often in or against dense foliage. As this habit often makes them difficult to see, it follows some distinctive sound should be consistently associated with their training at all stages.

One of the most serious problems regularly associated with these hawks is their reaction to being hooded. Buteos and falcons can be arbitrarily hooded without seriously affecting their attitude toward their trainer. However, this reaction is not the case with accipiters. An arbitrarily-hooded goshawk will, once it is unhooded, glare or scream and radiate hatred or fear for hours afterward. The bird is likely to show either resentment or apprehension of any motion of the hand which performed the unhooding for days or weeks thereafter. Repeated hooding also does not eventually result in resigned acceptance. To be hooded without offense, these hawks must be bribed and slowly persuaded to accept the hood. This bribery can be accomplished, but it requires the utmost time, care and patience.

Passage accipiters which are to be primarily flown across dry, open, or frozen terrain to upland game birds (quail, pheasant, gray partridge or chukar) or to rabbits or hares need no lure training. Goshawks, however, if they are to be later flown in forest areas or in hill country to ruffed, spruce or blue grouse, or across streams or ditches to waterfowl, do require lure training. Also, most eyesses require lure training, but for different reasons.

Training accipiters to the lure is primarily done to ensure long-distance recovery because they will seldom come back to the glove with any degree of reliability for distances in excess of about seventy yards. With the two small accipiters, recovery is usually no problem because they are seldom flown in the kind of terrain or to types of quarry which make long recoveries necessary. Lure-trained goshawks usually come straight back to the falconer from distances approaching a quarter mile which is no insignificant convenience in the field.

Some eyess accipiters, particularly eyess Cooper's hawks, which always have been fed on the glove, become what falconers term "fistbound." Such birds have come to regard the glove fist as their "prey" and of course, with "prey" already in their feet, they have no inclination to release the glove in pursuit of anything else. For such birds, the transfer of their concept of what constitutes "prey" from the glove to the lure is the only way they can be reoriented.

The introduction to the lure is no different for accipiters than for buteos, except with accipiters a winged lure should be used. As soon as they immediately fly from the glove to the lure the instant the latter is tossed out, the direction of the flight should be changed so it is again from a perch or from an assistant toward the falconer. However, the intent now is to initiate climbing strikes to the lure in midair. The techniques are illustrated. There is no need for an accipiter to be flown entirely free during this exercise even at this point, but if it is worked from a ground line, the lead to the hawk should be longer than is required for buteos. The lure should be pulled along the ground and the hawk should be permitted to take it once or twice, following which the speed of the lure is accelerated at the approach of the bird and, in one continuous motion, lifted and thrown up into the air behind the falconer. After a few repetitions of this action, the hawk will begin the flight toward the falconer the moment it sees the lure. The lure can then be tossed into the air between the falconer and the incoming hawk, as shown, with the resulting air-strike occurring, as a rule, almost directly above the falconer just as the lure stalls.

Following this practice, the hawk needs a further three or four days of training to the lure. On each day, the bird is taken to a different place where it is quietly carried about for half an hour or more before it is placed on a post or allowed to fly completely free to the limb of a tree. From there, it is called to the lure once or twice

145

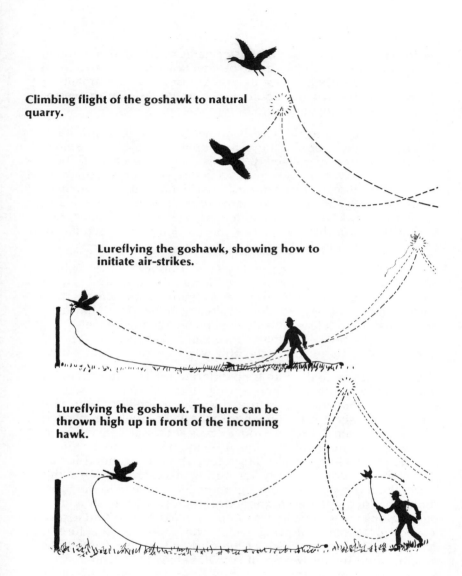

Climbing flight of the goshawk to natural quarry.

Lureflying the goshawk, showing how to initiate air-strikes.

Lureflying the goshawk. The lure can be thrown high up in front of the incoming hawk.

before being permitted to feed. During and after this period (with passage hawks, for a period of at least three months), a live lure should always be carried, but if possible, it should never be used. Showing the live lure is an almost infallible way to recover an accipiter. However, they are cunning birds and if they become aware the falconer will produce live quarry which they can always catch, they soon not only refuse to come to the falconer for anything less, but they also refuse to exert themselves in any stupid pursuit of free-flying quarries.

Because of the high degree of discernment which is characteristic of these hawks, entering procedures must be devious and cunning. They must always be arranged so the hawks cannot detect human hands have released the quarry which suddenly appears. The use of an assistant to release the quarry at a prearranged distance on a signal is an excellent strategem if the assistant is always concealed. The worst possible procedure is for the falconer to attempt a sneaky reach into the hawking bag to obtain and to release a quarry with the right hand while carrying the hawk on the left hand. Quarry released this close to an accipiter is instantly and invariably caught. This release procedure has only to happen twice before the hawk will focus its future attention on any movement of the falconer's right hand, a result which is not desirable at all.

With accipiters, the purpose of entering is as much to train the bird to treat the falconer as a mere slow-moving perch from which to watch the field as it is to orient the bird to any particular kind of quarry.

Because of their low tendency to take a "set," any strong-flying bird can be used if it is a size appropriate to the species of accipiter in training. It is important on these initial flights that the quarry be caught. The flight must go some distance and the quarry should vigorously fly with no appearance of being handicapped. Quarry used for entering flights should, therefore, be attached to a strong, lightweight and carefully-coiled line some fifty to seventy yards in length. The release should be sudden, effected through either a completely-hidden assistant or a hidden electric trap or trip-line spring-box. Any of these devices must be placed so the quarry, when it is released, appears to the hawk to have been naturally flushed from a ditch or a thicket some fifteen or twenty yards diagonally ahead and to the right of the falconer.

Two or three arranged successes of this kind, with the hawk permitted to kill and to eat to repletion from the first quarry and allowed decreasing portions of subsequent quarries, will show results. The hawk becomes unmindful of the falconer, but it is alert and it is watchful of the surrounding terrain. The hawk is then ready for the field.

ADVANCED TECHNIQUES

Now some comments on the more advanced training techniques are warranted. It soon comes to the attention of anyone seeking regular field-flights with these hawks, despite their capability of rapid acceleration, some birds such as pheasant, grouse and quail usually are their match or their superior. Two advanced training techniques which are designed to give the hawk the additional impetus needed for consistent success with these quarries have been in use for centuries in Asia.

By repetitive direct handling, the smaller accipiters can be conditioned to being held in the palm of the hand, breast downward, with their feet drawn back behind the thumb and forefinger encircling the bird at the base of the tail. From this position, the bird can be cast forward like a spear when quarry is flushed. The technique is applicable only to relatively small hawks. Sharp-shinned hawks and the males of the North American Cooper's hawk are within this size range.

THE HALSBAND

The use of a halsband produces much the same launching effect with larger accipiters. A halsband is a light-leather thong (for goshawks, it is some four inches in length) with a three to four inch diameter loop at one end. The loop is dropped over the head of the bird so it encircles the neck just ahead of the wings. In this position, it is worn with the loose end hanging down along the breast. Training an accipiter to the halsband is generally impractical unless pointing dogs are also used to locate quarry, in which case the hawk should become accustomed to the presence of dogs. Use of the halsband requires the falconer to have some foreknowledge about which quarry is to be flushed. The hawk is carried on the gloved hand in the usual way until quarry is located. Once quarry is located, the loose end of the halsband is drawn downward with the right hand until the hawk is nearly horizontal. It is held in this position by gripping the taut halsband with the gloved hand. The flush is then signalled. At the moment of the flush, the hawk is thrown forward with a horizontal sweep of the left arm. Without the halsband, the hawk would be tipped over backwards; with the halsband, the hawk is launched right at the quarry.

The halsband, to show how an accipiter can be held in the horizontal position preparatory to being thrown toward a quarry.

Where forest grouse inhabit level woodlands free of dense underbrush, some goshawks can be trained to hunt in trees from a position high above the falconer. Setting it free in the woodlands and releasing a quarry right under it first trains the bird to attend the falconer. The quarry is later released less overtly while making a great commotion in a thicket or when running. The association of the moving human having something to do with game being flushed is quickly made. This specialized training is best suited to eyess goshawks which usually like to keep the falconer in sight at all times. Attempts to train passage hawks this way, even when they are successful, are subject to a much higher risk of loss.

Few of the foregoing techniques are advisable for the novice. However, the throwing of a small accipiter from the right hand is always a possibility even for a beginner, especially when the hawk being trained is an eyess.

DISEASE

For some unknown reason, goshawks, more than any other birds of prey captured during migration, tend to be diseased. Frounce and aspergillosis are the pathogens most commonly encountered. While detailed discussion of the nature of these diseases and their treatment is out of place here, the distinctive behavior of infected birds is of primary concern when attempting to initiate training.

Healthy passage goshawks are always spare and are often thin, but they show great interest in food. Even those birds which at first refuse to feed from the glove in dim light will ravenously feed the moment they sense they are alone. The fact jesses and a leash restrain the birds does not inhibit them in the least. Birds with frounce are often starving and ravenously hungry. Frounce is usually easy to detect in most individuals because infected birds appear to be messy when they are feeding, this because little food can be swallowed due to a malfunction of the tongue. Pieces of meat torn from a carcass appear to cling the beak until they are flung aside and more is torn off, which also clings. Frounce can be quickly and easily cured. The drug known as emytryl is dramatically effective. (Note: Emytryl is no longer available and has been replaced by Flagyl.)

Individuals with pathogenic aspergillin infection usually have three well-marked characteristics. The first and the most obvious is an appearance of tameness and of unconcern. At the same time, despite being thin and underweight, when they are offered food they are offered food they feed indifferently if at all and they soon appear satisfied. They tend to sit erect with their feathers loose and fluffy; nothing seems to alarm or to excite them. Accipiters which exhibit this combination of characteristics immediately after being capture are usually doomed birds. Eventually, over a time-span which varies from two or three days to as long as three weeks, they will cease feeding altogether. Then, twenty-four to forty-eight hours later, they quietly fall from their perch, dying as they fall. Aspergillosis is difficult to treat and is nearly always fatal because its onset is so insidious it usually escapes notice until much too late.

HARRIS'S HAWKS

Harris's hawks can be trained either as buteos or as accipiters, or perhaps more correctly as primarily oriented to rabbits or to birds. As a rule, the females make more effective rabbit hawks and the tiercels make more effective bird-hawks. Most of the techniques outlined for the training of bird-oriented accipiters are directly applicable to the training of a bird-oriented Harris's hawk. However, some of the problems associated with accipiters, such as their unforgiving resentment of being hooded and their susceptibilities to aspergillosis and to frounce, are unlikely to be encountered.

Falcons

Falcons are the "noble hawks" of English and northern European literature. Throughout most of European medieval history, the ownership of falcons was restricted to the aristocracy, not as a conservation measure, as historically ignorant or propaganda-oriented contemporary conservationists have all too frequently implied, but as an arbitrary dictate of unabashed greed. The concern was with the protection of special class privilege, not the protection of falcons. When one compares the focus of attention given, research money spent and legislation academics and professionals imposed relative to falcons over the past decade with the parallel lack of attention and concern about hawks, one must wonder if the real concern has changed much.

Falcons are seldom the most effective of trained raptors, but they are definitely the most spectacular. It is the flare and the drama inherent in their hunting style which makes them so different from other raptors and which has for so long captured human imaginations and emotions.

FLIGHTS

The simplest flights of falcons are direct pursuits which differ only in being of longer duration and in covering greater distances than similar flights of accipiters. For these direct-chase flights, the procedures of training scarcely differ from those outlined for accipiters, except with falcons hooding is mandatory from the onset of training.

The "ringing" or "great" flights of antiquity are derived from direct pursuits and are due to the habit of some kinds of open-country birds to seek escape from any attacking raptor by contesting with it the mastery of the air. The ancients considered some of these flights, at which gyrfalcons excell, to be the ultimate in falconry. Training for such flights involves procedures which go beyond the training of accipiters.

Finally, and to some extent derived from the "ringing" flights, though the end result is dissimilar, are the anticipatory or "waiting on" flights. As already described, the falcon goes high aloft above the trainer when no quarry is in sight, but the movement is in expectation of quarry being "served." This flight is one to which other species can be trained with varying success, but one at which peregrines excell. It is this flight which is now considered the ultimate in falconry. For such flights, training involves still further techniques.

HOODING THE FALCON

The onset of training parallels that outlined for buteos and for accipiters, except for the necessity of hooding. Briefly, the falcon is picked up from half an hour to ten minutes before the training period, hooded and either carried about or just let sit while hooded. It is unhooded at the training site and it is called either from an assistant or from a post-perch to the glove. With falcons, this rudimentary training can be much foreshortened, both in the distance the bird is required to come and in the time spent. Three or four flights of only fifteen or twenty feet repeated only two or three successive days are adequate, following which the bird should be introduced to the lure.

AERIAL LURES

An aerial, winged lure should be used and, to begin with, the same procedures followed as those detailed for accipiters. The falcon is again unhooded on the glove in the training area so it may find the lure with the food attached already in its feet. Immediately, once it has begun to feed, the lure and the food are quickly and forcibly taken away and tossed to the ground. Shortly after this stage, the falcon can be unhooded and called to the lure as it flies down a ground line for distances of some thirty yards.

The preceding sequence may be reversed. Initiating the feeding from the lure at the onset of training may produce faster progress with wild-caught falcons. In this sequence, a lure with a full ration attached is placed on the ground beside the unhooded falcon either inside a building or outside near the lawn-perch. The falconer at once leaves the area and permits the falcon to take a full meal from the lure without any interference.

The next day at the same time and place, a lure with a full ration attached is placed beside the falcon in exactly the same way. However, this time the falconer, although he may go some thirty yards or more distant, remains in sight. As soon as the falcon begins feeding, the falconer moves closer until he comes as close as the bird will tolerate and will still continue to feed. This practice continues on subsequent days until the falcon is indifferent to the presence of the falconer either standing or kneeling close beside it.

When it reaches this stage, hooding and ground-line flights are begun. These ground-line flights must be continued with falcons until they permit the falconer to pick up them and the lure together and stand upright with them still unconcerned and still feeding from the lure. Only then may the next step be undertaken with any degree of composure.

It is at this point the training of falcons abruptly diverges from the procedures detailed for other raptors. To comply with their natural inclinations and their natural flight-style, they must now be flown completely free. Such first flights can be critical with passage falcons and the help of an assistant will greatly reduce the risk of loss. It is important the falcon see and pay attention to the lure before being permitted to fly. When a bird is unhooded and is set atop a post, there is no assurance he will pay attention to the lure, but if an assistant holds and unhoods the bird, the hold on the jesses can be maintained until the attention of the bird is clearly on the lure prior to its release.

On the first free flight, the lure should merely be dragged along the ground, as before, and the falcon permitted to land upon it. Both should be picked up together, the falcon fed a bite or two and then the lure taken away as it is returned to its original position. The lure should immediately be tossed out again and dragged along the ground, but this time the lure must be accelerated, lifted and swung away from the bird as it approaches. The lure is not tossed up ahead, as with an accipiter, but it is swung up and aside so the falcon misses and flies past in a climbing curve. As the bird gains height and comes around, the lure should at once be presented again and the falcon permitted to land upon it. The next step, a day later, is to make it miss and circle twice; the following day the bird is forced to circle three or four times. Following this procedure, on about the fourth or the fifth day of free-flying, comes the next and, for many novices, the most difficult step — the beginning of real lure flying.

LURE FLYING

The purpose of lure flying is to give a falcon exercise which develops a strong-flying, well-conditioned bird. Lure flying can be effective only to the extent it parallels and compliments the natural flight-style of the falcon when it is in pursuit of game. Good lure flying can itself develop a good field falcon, but sloppy and ill-timed luring can actually be detrimental.

The illustrations show the natural flight line of attacking falcons which luring must simulate to be of any use. As long as the lure is presented to the bird in such a way it tends to stimulate the type of attack which is natural, the falcon will pursue the lure in much the same style it normally shows when in pursuit of wild quarry. The attack from below in a steep climb to a lure tossed up in front of

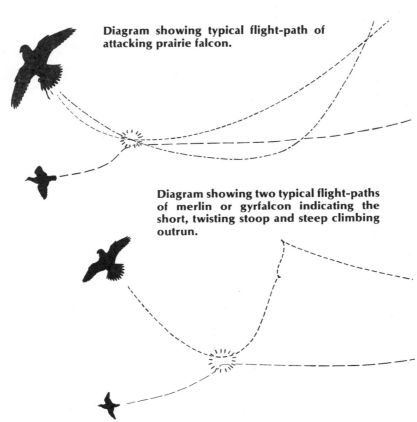

Diagram showing typical flight-path of attacking prairie falcon.

Diagram showing two typical flight-paths of merlin or gyrfalcon indicating the short, twisting stoop and steep climbing outrun.

them, while a good technique for accipiters, is upside-down for falcons because they always try to place themselves above and behind a quarry. The lure must be presented to falcons in such a way as to encourage and not to frustrate their downward style of attack.

Merlins, prairie falcons and gyrfalcons, while they regularly attack their prey from above, usually do not come down from great heights. These falcons accordingly fly well to the lure. For peregrines, the discipline of lure flying, however necessary, can never exactly parallel their natural method of taking prey. Thus, in this exercise they usually appear less spectacular and less energetic than other species.

The technique of hand-luring is illustrated. It is simple enough in theory, but hand-luring requires good co-ordination combined with equally good judgment of speed and of distance. The lure-line should be slightly shorter than double the distance of the out-stretched arms and, because the lure requires a drag and because the falconer's glove is adequate for this purpose, the free end of the

Long-line luring from (a) above and (b) the side showing how the lure is presented to stimulate the natural attack-style of the falcons. Dotted line indicates typical flight-path of gyrfalcon or merlin.

line should be tied or be snapped to the glove. The right hand holds the line about midway between the glove and the lure. The lure is then swung in a clockwise (viewed from below) circle at an angle of about forty-five degrees to the horizontal with the low point of the circle being diagonally in front and to the left of the falconer.

Some practice in lure-handling should precede any attempt to initiate air-strikes to the moving lure. If the initial passes of the falcon to the lure on the ground have been made with the lure pulled away from the falcon in the direction now indicated, the continuation of the movement results in the lure flying the course desired when it is kept in continuous motion.

With the falcon released and flying, the falconer must then try to correlate the constantly changing position of the lure to the constantly changing position of the falcon. At the same time, he must anticipate the intent of the falcon so when the bird lines up, accelerates and comes in relative to the lure at a correct distance, the lure-line is let slide through the fingers to lengthen the line at the same time the lure sweeps low to the ground ahead of, and below, the incoming falcon. As the lure comes into this position, the falcon will further accelerate and attempt to strike or to grab it as it moves along the flattened arc which the lengthened line

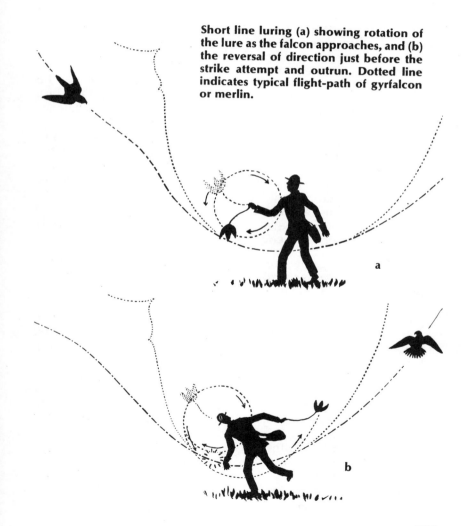

Short line luring (a) showing rotation of the lure as the falcon approaches, and (b) the reversal of direction just before the strike attempt and outrun. Dotted line indicates typical flight-path of gyrfalcon or merlin.

a

b

causes. Abruptly shortening the line arranges misses, increases the speed and tightens the curve of the lure as it comes around and up. This shortening of the line also carries the falcon up almost as if it was attached to the lure and carries it on past in a fast curving outrun. Lengthening the line to the limit arranges strikes as it slows its speed and straightens its course.

POLE LURING

An alternative, and in some ways a more effective, technique of lure-training is done with the use of a lightweight pole. A fiberglas fishing rod "blank" (a rod before it is fitted with line-guides) of the size used for tuna fishing makes an excellent lure-pole. The line which connects the lure to the pole should be about six inches shorter than the pole and about one-sixteenth of an inch thick. This size ensures the bird will see the line and prevents the line from cutting the bird if the two should accidentally make contact. With this arrangement, it will be found a lightweight lure can be controlled with the utmost precision. Most novices find the lure much easier to control this way. In addition, many passage falcons are less apprehensive of striking a lure when it is well removed from the falconer than when it is nearby. Some eyesses are almost impossible to persuade to take the lure in motion without the slow-motion precision which the use of the pole permits. Pole-luring causes the lure to move through the air for greater distances at a higher speed than is possible to attain with a hand-lure. Therefore, falcons flown to it tend to fly higher and faster. This training has no adverse effect; a hand-held lure is perfectly adequate later for the recovery of the falcon in the field.

The days which follow are a period of adjustment between the falcon and the falconer. With a novice, days or even weeks may pass before the degree of skill which permits the falconer to control a miss or a strike is acquired. The reason for attaching the lure to the glove becomes apparent in this interval because the falcon will soon try to snatch the lure at full speed. When this flight occurs, the falconer can let go of everything and permit the trailing, flopping glove (or released pole) to bring the falcon down. As soon as the bird and the falconer have reached the degree of co-ordination where the falcon is flying from four to ten passes and regularly taking the lure in motion, the practice of sitting the bird on an alternative perch can be discontinued and the falcon can be simply unhooded and put into the air; in falconry terms, the bird is "cast off" into the wind with a forward sweep of the arm. With peregrines, prairie falcons and eyesses of all falcons, this cast off can be done before the lure is produced because the two species always circle while eyesses always show concern for the where-abouts of their trainer.

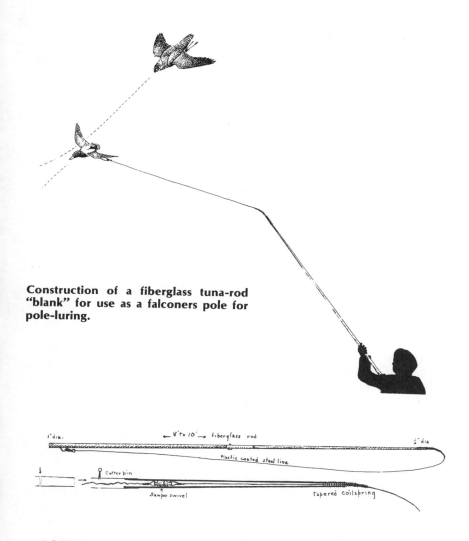

Construction of a fiberglass tuna-rod "blank" for use as a falconers pole for pole-luring.

1" dia.   ←— 8' to 10' —→ fiberglass rod   ½" dia.

Plastic coated steel line

Cotter pin

Sambo swivel   Tapered coilspring

LOSSES

Passage gyrfalcons and merlins can be suddenly and permanently lost at this stage of training, especially those birds which belong to falconers who have some experience with other species. The loss occurs because gyrfalcons and merlins have no inherent tendency to circle; after being suddenly unhooded and cast off, they may go straight away from the falconer. When this problem occurs they often keep going until they are out of sight — a most disconcerting misadventure, particularly to an "experienced" falconer. The lure must always be produced and be shown to these falcons before they are cast off during the entire early period of training to the lure.

CALLING OFF

When a falcon has progressed to where it will continuously fly for eight or ten consecutive passes and the falconer has progressed to where he is in control of passes or of strikes, two final procedures will result in a greatly-reduced risk of later loss if they are introduced at this stage. While falcons naturally pay far less attention to sound than do accipiters, they do hear well and learn to make sound associations. Therefore, if a single loud blast is sounded on a whistle just before the final contact-strike to the lure is permitted, a meaningful association with this sound to the reward will soon be established.

Immediately following this stage (it needs to be done only two or three times), the final training procedure known as "calling off" can proceed. Calling off is begun as a repetition of the initial stage of training where an assistant holds the hooded falcon. It is then unhooded and it is permitted to fly to the falconer. Now the intent is to train the bird further in associating the sound of the whistle to the man with the lure. Initially, the assistant takes the falcon a distance of only 100 or 150 yards (100 or 150 meters) where it is unhooded in clear sight of the falconer. The falconer then sounds the whistle just once and immediately swings the lure. The falcon of course responds and, after completing the required number of passes, is permitted to take the lure. The whistle is again sounded as it does so. Following this pass, the distance between the assistant and the falconer is regularly and rapidly increased on subsequent days until the falcon is flying a lineal distance of a half-mile or more. Since this kind of training is most effective and the risk of loss is reduced if the bird is exercised either early or late in the day, care should be taken so the flights are made with the assistant either having his back to the sun or at right angles to the sun. Toward the end of this period, which should last at least two weeks, the assistant should seek prearranged positions out of sight of the falconer, but where the falcon, upon hearing the whistle, can bring him into view as it circles upward. Until the distance between the assistant and the falconer has been increased to about one half-mile, it is scarcely necessary for the assistant to carry a lure. During the latter part of this training, however, especially when the bird is being trained to seek the unseen falconer from a considerable distance across unfamiliar terrain, the assistant must not only carry a lure, but he also must carry a whistle and be prepared to call the bird down should it begin to wander wide or set off in a wrong direction.

All this latter advanced training is intended to facilitate the field recovery of a falcon which has been taken, in the course of a long flight to quarry, an unknown distance from the falconer in a direction not precisely known. Two types of flights which regularly take falcons for distances in excess of a mile from their starting point (which at eye-level is out of human sight) are direct chases to fast, low-flying upland game birds such as pheasant, sharp-tailed grouse, chukar or ptarmigan and the high "ringing" flights to species which seek escape in the sky. These ringing flights sometimes drift considerable distances downwind. The calling off procedure is particularly necessary for falcons intended for either of these flights.

ENTERING

The final phase of training is, of course, entering. Falcons always tend to make a "set" to some particular type, sometimes even to a particular species or sex, of quarry — which means they like to become repetitive specialists in a particular type of flight. Therefore, a falcon entered to and given experience and success in direct pursuits of upland game birds will not fly crows while a falcon which has learned the tricks and the aerial strategy required to take crows is not inclined to deliver the amount of sheer physical exertion required to overhaul or to exhaust a pheasant or a chukar. Furthermore, any falcon which has learned the really easy way of taking prey by means of a swift, devastating plunge from high aloft is forever after disinclined to exert itself much on either of the other flights.

Therefore, entering should be made to a particular type or even a particular species of quarry. Entering flights should simulate as closely as possible the natural conditions, except for the arrangements which ensure these flights are successful. In entering a large falcon for either direct or for ringing flights (or in entering a merlin, tiercel peregrine or tiercel prairie falcon to smaller flocking species such as starlings), the quarry need not be hidden. This difference is because the falcon will be brought within easy flight-distance before it is unhooded and many natural flights later will start in exactly this way; that is, the falconer sees quarry on the ground in the open some distance away, approaches it and unhoods his falcon. Under field conditions later on, many flights to upland game may indeed be to birds which jump into startled flight nearer at hand. A falcon already entered to upland game will pursue these birds willingly enough.

Upland game birds of all kinds are palatable to falcons, as are starlings and all birds such as grackles, blackbirds and cowbirds which resemble starlings in size and often associate with them. If, prior to being entered, the falcon has not been permitted to pluck and to eat such a bird, this step should now be the first step in training. A dead bird of the appropriate kind can be simply substituted for the lure at the end of a routine lure-flight. If, as with a pheasant, the complete carcass is large enough to allow gorging, most of the meat should be removed so the weight of the meat on the carcass approximates the weight of the regular daily food intake. The following day, the falcon should be unhooded some ninety-nine to 165 feet (thirty to fifty meters) away from a live bird of the same kind which is tethered to the ground. The falcon is permitted to capture and to kill the bird, but it is allowed to eat only the normal weight of food, although it may be given the severed wings to pluck and to dismember further after the bulk of the carcass has been removed.

Only one or two more entering flights are now needed. These flights must still be to tethered quarry, but now the tether is arranged so either the falconer or an assistant can quickly release the quarry at a signal from the falconer as soon as the falcon has attained flying speed and has covered half or more of the distance between the falconer and the quarry. When it is suddenly released, the tethered bird nearly always flies straight away from the falcon and is taken in the air only a short distance later.

WILD QUARRIES

Following one or two experiences of this kind, the falcon will fly wild quarries of the same or similar kind at every opportunity, although usually with only low to moderate success. With eyesses, it is often necessary to arrange successful kills from time to time during the entire first season in order to maintain the needed levels of enthusiasm and confidence which are the prerequisites for exciting flights to wild quarries.

Of the species of birds which go aloft in an attempt to seek escape from an attacking falcon, the common crow is the quarry most widely available. Flights to crows are possible only where they regularly occur in situations far from brush or trees. The corvids generally, and the crows in particular, are not palatable to falcons; the humiliation implied in the term "eating crow" refers to this fact. While the entering procedures for crow falcons are no different from those already outlined, some modifications are necessary. Thus, in the first feeding, a black-plumaged, headless pigeon carcass, not that of a crow, should be used. The first tethered crow should have its beak tied shut so it cannot bite and, immediately after the falcon has made the kill and begun the depluming, a second black pigeon must be substituted. Finally, because any crow falcon is eventually sure to be bitten (to avoid this problem, the bird must learn to grip the crow around the head), there should be a short sequence of flights to released crows which carry a matchstick tied crosswise in their beaks so they can squawk as loud as they like and so they can bite a little, but so they are unable to get a really painful hold.

DOG, HORSE AND FALCON

The combination of pointing dogs and falcons in the capture of upland game birds is usually associated with falcons trained to "wait on." This combination is adaptable to some direct flights, particularly to those of gyrfalcons to pheasants and, in hill country, to downslope flights of any of the three large falcons to chukar. If these flights are contemplated, a casual, daily exposure of the falcon to the particular dog which will be involved over a considerable period of time is the first necessity. Once the falcon is indifferent to the near presence of the dog, the entering procedures can proceed exactly as they are detailed for the entering of an accipiter: the quarry is placed in a hidden spring-box (or a hidden assistant holds it), the dog is brought to point, the falcon is unhooded with the dog on point and the quarry is hurled into sudden flight. This procedure is altogether too complex for one man to attempt alone. In all cases where the use of dogs and falcons together is contemplated, falconry becomes at least a two-person recreation.

The really ideal position from which to fly a falcon for either direct or for ringing flights is from the saddle on the back of a good mount. The mounted falconer, provided he is a good rider and he has access to an area free of fences and ditches, can follow out direct flights at a speed approaching about one-third of the falcon and he can easily keep pace with most ringing flights. Indeed, most of the training procedures detailed here (except pole-luring) are only minor modifications of ancient techniques which mounted men originally devised. Currently, however, few falconers are so situated as to make the classic combination of horse, man and falcon a practical possibility.

THE PEREGRINE

Contemporary western falconers usually consider the training of a peregrine to climb to and to hold a lofty position in the air above the falconer in the expectation of quarry being "served" the ultimate achievement in falconry. With much diligence and much repetition, some individuals of other species can also be trained to perform this way, but it is a discipline which comes naturally only to peregrines. The actual training of most peregrines to "wait on" is a task of no great difficulty. The practicability of going to the expense and the trouble of getting a peregrine to train in this manner is another matter. These high flights are highly specialized and they are suitable only to limited kinds of quarry, or, at times, to a somewhat broader range of quarries under special conditions. Moreover, for reasons not at all apparent to the novice and difficult to explain, though they are immediately discernible in the field, the advantage the falcon gains is not nearly as great as the human mind always imagines. Under many conditions, the training of a peregrine to "wait on" will turn out to be either an exercise in futility or a sad perversion of field falconry.

Far too often the North American falconer, bemused with the doubtful double glamor of the "noble" peregrine and its fabled "stoop," expects his falcon to go high aloft and to wait on as steadily and as patiently as a kite on a string while he, with no help from pointing dogs or even spaniels and often with no assurance any kind of game is nearby, runs around kicking grass-tussocks or dashing into thickets in hope of making something — well, anything — fly out. The most amazing thing about this kind of performance is the length of time some peregrines do hang over him. However, under these conditions, even the best of them eventually lose height, go clear out of sight, drift wide or drift downwind and have to be called down to the lure.

WILD QUARRIES

North America produces an enviable range of quarries well suited for high-flying peregrines, although some of these quarries do not always occur under conditions where they can be taken. The detailed procedures of field falconry are discussed in the next chapter, but the following is a list of North American game-bird species which, if they are available under the right conditions, can be consistently taken. These bird species are: Wilson's snipe, mourning dove, bobwhite quail, Gambel's quail, California quail, European gray partridge, chukar partridge, pinnated grouse, sharp-tailed grouse, willow ptarmigan, coot, green-winged, blue-winged and cinnamon teal, shoveller, gadwall, widgeon and pintail.

The following species and groups, despite appearances or stories to the contrary and disregarding the fact wild peregrines regularly take some, are difficult and unsuitable for trained peregrines. These species and groups are: all the "protected" migratory passerines except for the meadowlarks, all the shorebirds and the plovers except for the Wilson's snipe, all the "diving" ducks such as the bufflehead, scaup and canvasback, sage-grouse, blue-grouse, spruce, Franklin's and ruffed grouse, rock ptarmigan, white-tailed ptarmigan, pheasant and mallard.

Only the placing of the last two species in the second — unsuitable — group can be questioned. These two species admittedly are borderline, but cock pheasant and mallard drakes are too big and too strong for most female peregrines and far too large for tiercels.

All the procedures detailed for the training of pursuit falcons are perfectly applicable to peregrines trained for waiting on flights. Even the long-distance calling off exercise can prove to be well-spent time, although the problems of recovery following an unsuccessful flight and of location following a successful flight are considerably less because flights usually terminate much closer to the falconer. The training of a falcon which is to "wait on" diverges and requires different techniques than previously outlined at the point of entering. Here, the falconer must make some firm decisions because once the falcon is past a certain point in training it is pretty much committed and unlikely to be changed.

RELEASE-QUARRIES

Because peregrines are even more inclined than most other falcons to take a set to whatever type of quarry they are successfully entered upon, the problem is to acquire a considerable number of suitable quarries. The training to wait on is a repetitive procedure which requires a steady supply of release quarries. Not all of the quarries are likely to be taken, but all of them must be expendable. The requirement is the falcon be served at least one strong, free-flying quarry every time it is unhooded and it is flown free in order for the bird to learn, through repetition, the advantage and the reward of holding a high position in the air above the falconer. The use of domestic pigeons as release quarries solves some of the problems and it is probably the easiest way to train a high-flying falcon, but this solution can result in a pigeon-set falcon which may itself prove to be a problem. Seldom, however, does the repeated use of domestic pigeons for training cause peregrines to ignore upland game. Falcons being trained for contemplated flights to meadowlark, mourning dove, Wilson's snipe, quail, gray partridge, chukar, sharp-tailed grouse or ptarmigan can usually be trained through the use of domestic pigeons without the loss of interest in these quarries in the field.

If, on the other hand, flights to waterfowl are contemplated, any use of pigeons should be avoided. Falcons so trained usually ignore waterfowl. Female peregrines trained to mallards from the beginning usually become among the most excellent field falcons because these birds will subsequently stoop with complete assurance to any of the upland game birds, even to pheasant and to sage-grouse. Falcons entered and repeatedly flown to ducks and, for that matter, falcons entered and repeatedly flown to upland game tend to ignore pigeons unless these birds are accidentally flushed or deliberately released right under them.

Generally speaking, if strong-flying, game-farm quarries other than pigeons are available to the falconer in sufficient numbers to permit repeated use, it is well to avoid using pigeons altogether. The pigeon-oriented falcons can be drawn by them into troublesome or into perilous situations. However, where peregrines are being primarily trained to take advantage of a short open season on upland game, the use of pigeons can have real merit because they permit the falconer virtually to fly his bird the year round and still have an effective field falcon.

Where flights to waterfowl are contemplated and semi-domestic or game-farm mallards are utilized as the release quarry, many of the same precautions should be taken as when entering a falcon to crows. Domestic mallards, particularly ducks, are often singularly aggressive. When the falcon captures them in flight, they usually give little trouble, but if they are knocked out of the air and they are not badly hurt, or if they refuse to fly (as they sometimes do), they then tend to attack the falcon if it attempts to grab them or lands nearby. A young falcon once mauled by a domestic mallard can seldom be persuaded to attack that kind of bird again. Wild mallards rarely react this way. Of the domestic mallards, the best variety to utilize for quarry is the small breed known to aviculturists as the "call duck."

ADVANCED TRAINING

Once the falcon has been entered, further training can proceed. There is a wide variation in the adaptability of different individuals to the discipline with passage birds usually responding better than eyesses and tiercels usually responding better than females. While it could be said a time period of at least two weeks and something in excess of fourteen release quarries are the minimum requirements, the fact is flight training never ends. Even for a falcon flying in the field in its third or in its thirty-third season, the falconer should carry live quarry with which to serve his falcon, unless it is flying marked game.

Simply unhooding and releasing the falcon and letting it fly about begins its training. No attempt need be made to have the first stoops come from any great height. Eyesses are best taken either to a perfectly flat area free of elevated perches such as utility poles or fenceposts, or to an open flat backing against the abrupt slope of a hill which has an upslope breeze blowing. The latter type of area should be avoided with a passage bird. If eyesses are used, they are unhooded and they are released without being showed the lure in the hope they will fly about and come above the falconer. Passage birds are less inclined to perch and they are also less inclined to pay much attention to the falconer at first. With these birds, it is often better to give them a glimpse of the lure either just before or just after they are cast off. On the early flights, the quarry should be served at the first opportunity. As soon as the falcon comes even a little upwind of and above the falconer and it has begun to turn back downwind over level ground, the quarry is thrown out downwind from the hand of the falconer. With a bird riding an upslope wind, the flight will be at right angles to the slope and directly into the wind. While success on the first two or three such flights is important, balanced against this success and equally important is the fact the quarry should not only be taken in the air, but it should also appear to fly normally. Strong-flying quarries which are deviously handicapped are, therefore, much better for training than are weak or immature quarries which soon flutter to the ground. Pigeons hence are the most-commonly used quarry. The best way to handicap quarry is to equally shorten both wings so the released bird does not fly with a list. Another kind of handicapping can be accomplished if the bird has one eye covered, which causes the bird to fly in a circle, or if the bird has both eyes shielded from behind so it is unaware of the falcon and unable to dodge effectively. The release of quarries attached to anchored lines is dangerous for the falcon because it can badly cut itself on the lines, but with small release quarries there is sometimes a real advantage in having them trail three to six meters of light line. Not only does this line act as a handicap, the falconer may also grasp it when he approaches a falcon on the ground with its prey in order to prevent the falcon from flying off with the quarry.

This last hazard is one of the best reasons for utilizing large, heavy quarries for the early flights, particularly when you are training passagers. While a tiercel peregrine can indeed carry an average-size domestic pigeon, it usually finds it troublesome and tends to stay in one place. However, a female can easily carry a pigeon and most passage falcons, when they annex a pigeon in midair, are quite inclined to do so. It takes a bird of hen pheasant-size to bring these birds to the ground while no peregrine gets anywhere at all if fast to a bird the size of a mallard.

Except for flights to waterfowl, the ultimate combination of desirata in the trained "waiting on" falcon remains constant: the falcon must learn to associate the position of the falconer with the sudden appearance of the quarry; for this reason, it must learn to circle above the falconer; it must learn its best chance of taking quarry is to hit it hard or to seize it at the termination of the first or the second stoop; finally, it must learn to abandon pursuit the moment it flattens out into a direct chase.

To accomplish all these necessities, the falconer should be familiar with the different behavior characteristics of the different types of release quarries when these are under stress. Of the three types of domestic or game-farm quarries, the upland, short-winged game-birds are easily the most likely to be regularly captured. They are, therefore, the least likely to result in lost falcons or in flights which go out of sight. The problem here is not in the likelihood of these birds flying too far, but in the difficulty of obtaining birds of this type which will competently fly. Passage falcons usually kill released game-farm birds of this type much too regularly and much too easily. Wild, upland game birds which have been trapped do, however, fly well and, if they can be obtained, they are much better quarries, particularly for passage falcons or for the later training of eyesses. For the best results, all upland game bird releases should be made at distances of no more than 100 yards (100 meters) from some easily visible form of dense cover such as a patch of woods, a dense sizeable thicket or a standing crop. This type of area generally results in the release quarry making a co-ordinated effort to escape by reaching the cover. Whether the quarry makes its escape or not, the result is a good training flight which is quickly and predictably terminated.

Domestic pigeons always fly well because it is their nature to attempt to escape from a falcon in the air, first dodging and then outflying or overclimbing their pursuer. Falconers highly favor pigeons because they are the most dependable, most available and most predictable of training quarries. However, these same characteristics can easily result in lost falcons because pigeons are hard for falcons to hit and many flights quickly degenerate into the tailchase. Pigeons trapped at random in cities or in towns and released under the falcon in strange terrain tend to take a falcon out of sight straightaway unless some precautions are taken. Covering one eye of the pigeon with a lightly-adhered patch of brown paper gummed tape will usually cause it to circle to hold the flight nearer at hand. If such a pigeon takes the falcon high aloft, a second pigeon released just as the falcon abandons pursuit of the first will bring the falcon down onto the second. This action also serves as excellent training. The safest and the most effective pigeons for training a falcon are those which are released under the falcon when they are within a half-mile radius of their own home loft. Such pigeons may also attempt to outfly the falcon, but while they may circle and take it high aloft, they immediately become oriented to their known refuge if they are hit, outflown or hard-pressed. Whether they make it to the home loft of the pigeon or not, the falconer knows where they are going and the exact point at which an unsuccessful tailchase will terminate.

Wild-trapped waterfowl, when they are released, fly as strongly and as predictably as domestic pigeons, but they are less adept at dodging and they are more likely to be hit. If they are not hit and they get up to full speed, they regularly pull away from any eyess and even from many passage falcons. The potential for taking a falcon over the horizon is much the same for waterfowl as with pigeons which are trapped and are randomly released. Game-farm mallards or call-ducks do not usually fly nearly so well and unless they are given some kind of sanctuary, they may be too regularly caught in the tailchase. The powers of flight encountered later in the chase to waterfowl make this result most undesirable. Releasing ducks within a half-mile of a fair-sized, visible sheet of water obtains the best results. This release quickly orients the ducks every time as it gives them a predictable distance, direction and termination point for unsuccessful flights.

During the early stages of training, up to the time when the falcon becomes reasonably predictable in its orientation to the falconer, the release quarries can be served openly and even overtly. However, there comes the time when this practice also must cease. If this practice is continued too long, it results in a beautifully steady, high-flying falcon which will steadfastly ignore all quarries not originating from the falconer's right hand. Hidden assistants and covertly-placed electronic or trip-line spring-boxes, therefore, have their place in the later stages of the training of a high-flying peregrine (particularly of an eyess) if a competent field bird is to be produced. In this area of discussion, however, waterfowl are again the exception. In the field, waterfowl are never sprung from hidden places, they are always sprung from positions on water in plain sight of the high-flying falcon. On waterfowl flights, it is best if the falcon learns to relate to the quarry's position rather than to the falconer's position. The closer the training releases can simulate this future field condition, the more effective they will be. A few domestic ducks in a small pond which do not fly along with the falconer splashing about in the same pond and hurling into flight one which does fly is a most effective kind of association in training.

Gyrfalcons, once they are unhooded and they are released, are so impatient to chase something they are nearly useless as high-waiting falcons for upland game, but they are wonderful duck falcons. With their quarry in sight, they quickly learn to place themselves over it, to circle it and to wait willingly for the rather short time the falconer requires to make the flush.

TOM W. HALL

Field Hunting

BUTEOS AND EAGLES

There is a saying amongst contemporary falconers that "those who fly hawks have all the fun while those who fly falcons have all the problems." This saying probably originated at one of the North American Falconry Association meets in South Dakota during the halcyon pre-regulation period of the mid-1960s. The observation was falconers who went out to the woodlots and to the fields carrying red-tails or Harris's hawks came back laden with slain quarry and they still carried their hawks. Those people who went out carrying one of the glamorous long-winged falcons sometimes returned with, at best, one or two head of quarry and their falcon, but they frequently came back with neither.

Nevertheless, comparisons in flights and in successes between species are more interesting and they are less disappointing if the falconer knows beforehand what he can expect of his bird in the field. There are comparatively few variables, for instance, in the short-distance flights of a Harris's hawk or a red-tail hawk. When the bird is released from the falconer's fist to pursue a cottontail rabbit flushed out ahead from a weedpatch or a brushpile, the flight is short and is quickly terminated. There is far more difficulty for the falconer attempting the forced flush of a pheasant at the exact moment most advantageous to a high-flying falcon. A comparison less obvious is one between the falconer carrying a red-tail or a Harris's hawk into the field and the falconer with a goshawk. The former can take his bird to seek quarry on strange terrain and in the company of strange people. He can be confident if a rabbit is jumped, the hawk will disregard everything but the rabbit. However, under identical circumstances, the falconer carrying a goshawk is never sure all the strange new sights and new sounds will not distract it from paying the slightest attention to a rabbit. Moreover, the goshawk in these circumstances will surely be difficult or perhaps impossible to recover if it is released.

RED-TAIL AND HARRIS'S HAWK

The effectiveness of Harris's hawks and red-tails is due as much to their unexcitable nature and their lack of suspicion as it is to anything else. While both, particularly the Harris's hawk, can sometimes catch birds in flight, neither is inclined to persist in aerial chase for long. Both species, following any unsuccessful chase, are inclined to perch in the open where they can be easily seen and easily recovered. Their use is free of most of the more irritating variables of behavior associated with other species. Falconers who fly these hawks in areas where ground quarries abound are

169

rewarded with plenty of action and with few problems.

Eyesses of either the Harris's hawk or the red-tailed hawk are seldom lost in the field, even temporarily. Even when they are lost, they can be recovered later, as a rule, in the same area when the condition, usually weather related, causing their loss has improved or has abated. The most frequent reason for losing passage red-tails is the result of flying the bird at a time of day or in an association of wind and topography conducive to soaring. The hawks certainly sense warm-air thermals as these develop on warm and relatively windless days. The hawks also sense the lift to the air which occurs wherever a steady breeze moves upslope or impinges against long lines of trees, cutbanks or cliffs. Some hawks encountering such weather conditions may soar aloft to great heights while others drift downwind. However, even when they drift, these hawks are seldom lost if they are anywhere within sight of areas they have previously flown over several times. Only when they inadvertently go soaring over areas completely new and completely strange to them is their loss likely to be permanent.

Falconers with some experience dealing with these species sometimes deliberately seek areas conducive to soaring when hunting with proven birds. The hawk is released and it is permitted to soar while the falconer, often in combination with a dog, seeks to rout out quarry. This method can result in a high-soaring hawk executing a spectacular falcon-like stoop to the quarry, usually to rabbit or to hare, but occasionally to birds.

Although usually flown across open fields, lightly treed parklands or small semi-open woodlots, both red-tailed hawks and Harris's hawks will pursue quarries in deep woods. Harris's hawks, because they are shorter of wing and they are quicker at making turns, are considerably more effective as forest hawks than are red-tails. Neither bird is lacking in courage and only the largest white-tailed prairie hares and the huge arctic hares are beyond their capabilities.

FERRUGINOUS HAWK AND GOLDEN EAGLE

Ferruginous hawks and golden eagles are the two North American raptors capable of taking larger to much larger quarries at longer range than either the red-tailed or the Harris's hawks.

The behavior, capabilities and mannerisms of these two species, both in the field and toward their trainer, are so similar they can be discussed together almost as if they were a single species. These similarities are all the more evident when one considers the differences in dimensions and weight between the male and the female ferruginous hawk are nearly the same as those between the female ferruginous hawk and the male golden eagle.

There is certainly no species of hare or of rabbit in North America, and probably in the world, which is beyond the capability of a healthy female ferruginous hawk. In practice, this capability means the only North American ground quarries to which a golden eagle can be trained which the smaller raptor cannot as effectively capture are foxes, coyotes, wolves and perhaps pronghorn antelope. One must add few people in contemporary North America are situated where wolf or where antelope could make even an occasional quarry for an eagle.

Both ferruginous hawks and golden eagles are at their best when they are flown over nearly treeless landscapes. If they are carried unhooded and they are permitted to fly at will, they may see and start for quarries at distances as much as a mile away with the pursuit flight going an indeterminate distance further. Of the birds of chase, only the large falcons so regularly and so rapidly cover comparable distances. To release a bird even as large and as visible as either of these birds on flights of such distances is practical only when the falconer is transported in the field either by a horse or by a wheeled vehicle. This type of transportation permits the falconer to follow such flights without physical exhaustion and at higher ground speeds than is otherwise possible. Traditionally, of course, golden eagles were always flown from the saddle. It still works out in practice to enjoy the full recreational potential of either a golden eagle or a ferruginous hawk, some method of transporting both the falconer and the birds prior to the flight and the falconer following out the flight is indeed necessary.

A more controlled way of hunting with eagles and ferruginous hawks is to hood them prior to the hunt and carry them, while they are hooded, to the field. When moving quarry is sighted, the birds are unhooded. No matter how far away, the quarry will immediately be discerned and immediately be pursued. The huntsman then joins the chase, keeping as close to his bird as the terrain and his transport permits. When handled this way, it will soon be found both golden eagles and ferruginous hawks will also try to capture any of the larger open-country game birds if they are permitted to make the attempt in their own way. They show little inclination to start from a perch in direct pursuit of flying birds, but if either of these raptors is immediately unhooded when a bird is flushed, they will watch the flying bird with concentrated attention and go after it if it is observed to alight. The approach is made at high speed. These surprise attacks frequently take hidden winged quarries on the ground. Under these circumstances, both species have some inclination for aerial pursuit of quarries flushed out ahead of them, but in these chases ferruginous hawks are much the more determined and persistent.

The great distances golden eagles and ferruginous hawks cover in flights is the usual cause of their loss, especially when the distance covered is combined with some unexpected obstruction to the direct passage of the falconer such as a fence, ditch, gully, canyon or unfordable stream. Of the two species, eagles are more inclined to soar; their tendency to soar at the termination of an unsuccessful chase is noteworthy. With a species so large, however, this characteristic is less distressing than it might at first seem because it takes them up to where they can see and where they can be seen which may sometimes expedite rather than delay their recovery.

Of the two species, the hawks are considerably easier to bring into keen hunting condition. The hawks are also swifter in level flight and they are considerably more inclined to chase birds. They are also, of course, much less dangerous to their trainer and to humans generally. This characteristic is due to the smaller size of hawks rather than any significant difference in their disposition. They are enough like golden eagles in training and in handling as to require similar caution and similar respect.

Accipiters

The accipiters combine some of the most desirable with some of the most annoying characteristics of all the huntsman's hawks. They are perhaps the most eager of all hawks to give chase; when in pursuit, they are swift, determined and incredibly agile. They can also be flown over almost any kind of terrain at any time of day. They seldom take a set and they are willing to pursue either birds or mammals with equal zest. Between the three species of accipiters, they can take every kind of winged game under the size of a goose and every kind of furred game under the size of a prairie hare. With such a list of capabilities, accipiters should be the most sought-after birds of chase. However, they are not because so often the degree of patience required to train and to hunt with these birds touches the limits of human forbearance.

Except in some areas of open country in central Asia and in southeastern Europe where goshawks were sometimes flown from the saddle, the accipiters have traditionally been the footman's hawk. The duration of time goshawks were the primary human method of capturing upland game birds is perhaps best indicated if it is pointed out virtually all the different breeds of dogs which have been developed as pointers or as setters, as well as most of the spaniels, were originally bred to work with men carrying goshawks, not with men carrying guns.

The traditional method of making an accipiter indifferent to distractions and more useful and easier to recover in the field was for the falconer to carry the bird unhooded on his gloved hand. In earlier times, goshawks were carried almost continuously amongst people, strange dogs, large domestic animals, wheeled carts, vehicles and other potentially frightening things until the hawk came to accept all these as merely part of the daily background. Contemporary social conditions, combined with the far greater number and diversity of potentially frightening things, usually preclude this approach for the contemporary falconer. About the best which can be done under current conditions is to accustom the bird to the kind of dog it will be hunted with, to make it accept the presence of one or two people other than the falconer when it is carried and, most important of all, get it used to being transported in a motor vehicle. Beyond these necessities, the contemporary falconer must be more concerned with avoiding unfamiliar or potentially frightening things than with attempting to condition the bird to all of them. Working with an accipiter which has been trained to the hood solves many problems because while this training in no way prevents unforeseen alarms in the field, it nevertheless does much toward preserving calm in transit. Also, the falconer out with an easily-hooded hawk can also avoid many potentially alarming or potentially unpleasant situations before they have time to develop.

"IN YARAK"

Accipiters, together with buteos and eagles, but not falcons, indicate important emotional states through their posture. The ancient East Indian term of "in yarak" has been added to the semantics of falconry for lack of any synonomous English word. The term "in yarak" is applied to any buteo, eagle or accipiter which shows, to anyone who has learned to interpret the meaning of its posture, it is eager to kill. The phlegmatic buteos and the eagles refuse to pursue, and usually even to fly, when they are not in yarak, but the more high-strung, excitable accipiters frequently start for quarry and then veer off to a perch when they are not in yarak. Once they are free of their trainer, their recovery is usually difficult and time-consuming; the bird may also be permanently lost. Some of the more defined and more typical yarak postures of these hawks are illustrated. There is wide individual variation, but it should be noted any buteo, eagle or accipiter which is emotionally eager to hunt assumes a vertical stance with its plumage loose and its beak closed. Any accipiter which rides the glove tight-plumaged and perched at an angle, or horizontally, with its beak half-open is not safe to release.

FLIGHTS AND QUARRIES

With accipiters, most flights start from the glove and most successful flights are short — they often go for no more than ten or twenty yards (ten or twenty meters). The easiest quarries for these birds are not rabbits and hares, but certain slow-flying birds such as short-eared owls, bitterns and rails which tend to lie concealed and which permit close approach before suddenly springing upward in

173

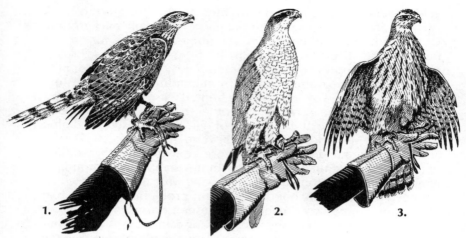

1. Horizontal position of a newly caught or frightened goshawk. Such a bird is unsafe to fly.

weak and wavering flight. Goshawks will take short-eared owls and Cooper's hawks will take burrowing owls before the owls scarcely clear the grass. So consistent are these successes that such flights are mere bloodlettings. Rails are just as easy for either species to take. Coots, surprised while feeding on the ground a few yards from water, also have no chance to escape. The diving ducks such as bufflehead and scaup, if they can be forced to fly out over land, provide a slightly more interesting flight; however, they also have poor acceleration. The active pond ducks such as mallard, widgeon and teal are more challenging. These ducks jump straight up out of the water, rapidly climb and have quick acceleration. They are also regularly found in small water areas such as ponds, ditches and streams where they can be covertly approached and startled into flight. Once surprised, they are either easy or they are difficult for an accipiter to take depending on how close an approach can be made before they flush. As a group, active pond ducks are excellent quarries for the two larger accipiters and they give exciting flights because they are usually taken often enough to build a high level of confidence in the hawk while they escape often enough to ensure variety.

One of the surprises of waterfowl flights lies in the number of times they terminate back in the water. Hawks initially underfly the fast-climbing duck to build up speed and then suddenly curve up to seize it from below at the limit of a nearly-vertical climb. Once fast to quarry of its own weight or more, the hawk with the quarry drop straight down. If the flight has gone out over, but not cleared, the water, it ends with both birds down in the water. Most

6. Extreme "yarak" position of a fist-bound Cooper's hawk.

4.

5.

6.

2-5. Variations in "yarak" posture of hunting goshawks. In all cases the position of the bird is almost vertical.

accipiters retain their hold long enough for the falconer to wade out and to lend assistance, provided the water is not too deep. The falconer must not grasp the hawk; he must reach underwater to grasp the duck and, thus, carry or toss both birds ashore. The hawk will retain its hold throughout if it is not touched. When flights terminate in deep water beyond help, the duck always escapes because the hawk must eventually let go or it will be pulled underwater. However, an accipiter down in the water and well out from shore is in no peril. As soon as the duck is released, the hawk will swim ashore with lunging wing strokes where, soggy, bedraggled and outraged, it can be easily picked up. The one drawback of any flight which ends on the water is further hunting is not possible until the hawk has preened and dried itself.

Flights with goshawks or with Cooper's hawks in woodlots or across pasturelands to cottontails, or with goshawks in open woods to snowshoe hares, do not significantly differ from flights to these same quarries with red-tails and with Harris's hawks. The same can be said of goshawk flights over sagebrush to black-tailed jack-rabbits and of Cooper's hawk flights in chaparral to western cottontails. Only in the last instance is the quick acceleration and agility of the accipiter of any significance to success. In calm weather, these quarries are overtaken so easily a goshawk which overflies a jackrabbit in sagebrush must reduce its normal speed to fly somewhat like a harrier in order to follow abrupt changes in direction. The strike, when it is made, is also harrier-like. In heavy sage growth, one strike usually ends the flight whether it is successful or not. The more direct flights to cottontails in fields or in woodlots, or to snowshoe hares in open woods, may result in two or three misses with the chase being instantly resumed after each miss. Some of these pursuits can also actively involve the falconer in routing out quarry which has found temporary shelter in weed-patch thicket or in brushpile. The hunting of cottontails in chaparral usually requires the help of either an assistant or a dog to force these brush rabbits to risk short dashes across small grassy openings.

Successful flights with accipiters to rabbits and to hares are not significantly more successful than the same flights with red-tails or with Harris's hawks; in situations where accipiters are likely to be exposed to anything strange or anything new, they may then be much less successful. However, when they are flown under these circumstances to ground quarries, the full capabilities of these hawks are not revealed.

GAME BIRDS

Pheasant, gray partridge, ruffed grouse, bobwhite and California and Gambel's quail are among the quarries wild goshawks and Cooper's hawks most avidly hunt wherever they occur together. These game species provide fascinating and varying flights because the accipiters are so attuned to these quarries even repeated failure never results in discouragement. The two groups appear to be bonded together in a long-established and a well-balanced predator-prey relationship. The explosive flush and the rocketing acceleration characteristics of the prey group have surely evolved as means of permitting the birds to cope successfully with the persistent and the sudden attacks of the accipitrine hawks. The immature poults of any of these prey species are consistently caught only a short distance from where any adult accipiter first flushes them. The adults and even the fully-plumaged young can hold their own, or even pull away from, a hawk not already in swift motion when such quarry is flushed. The ancient huntsman learned to hurl the sparrowhawk and he devised the halsband as a means of giving similar impetus to a goshawk in order to help it overcome such a handicap. As historical experience indicates, if accipiters are consistently to capture these game birds as they rise, some stratagems are essential. It is worth observing, however, practical men whose primary interest in the accipiter was not in recreation, but saw it as a means of obtaining game for market, devised these methods. The modern falconer who flies hawks for fun can arrange for his hawk to take these same quarries through other methods which produce far less game but which result in longer and in more interesting flights.

The group of upland game birds just listed, together with certain other hill-country species which will be discussed later, have evolved in a distinctive way. All these birds are like domestic fowl in that their breast musculature is pale pink when they are freshly skinned and it is white when they are cooked. The extremely rapid and extremely powerful contractions of the breast muscles which permit the explosive acceleration characteristic of these species is based on a different biochemical reaction than other game birds. These white breast muscles operate on chemically stored energy and they burn no oxygen in flight. This odd chemistry permits them to release a tremendous explosion of energy which is of short duration, but it is often sufficient to permit them to outdistance an accipitrine pursuer and to reach the safety of dense cover. The system works, but in releasing this stored energy these birds literally "burn out" because the energy in these muscles takes time to recharge. They would be secure from a wild hawk, but when a trained hawk flies them to cover, they are not safe. Shortly thereafter, and for the birds of this type far too soon, comes the falconer, or worse, the falconer and his dog while still perched "at mark" is the waiting, frustrated and far from exhausted hawk. Unless it is in deep and impenetrable cover, the quarry is now in real trouble. Sometimes the dog catches it and sometimes the falconer picks it up, but if it is forced to fly a second time, the hawk is always sure to catch it.

Flights of equal or of greater interest can be obtained when an accipiter is trained to follow the falconer by flying from tree to tree in the forest or if the accipiter has learned to identify the calls of partridge or quail and is permitted to fly toward the sounds in order to take perch above the quarry. Flights from the trees to woodland grouse almost exactly duplicate the natural flights of wild accipiters to the same quarry; the bird similarly cast off to take perch over coveys of quail results in the same type of flight as soon as the quail are flushed. Finally, where waterfowl can be seen on small tree-fringed ponds or creeks, these hawks will also learn to fly ahead of the falconer, to take perch above the quarry and to await eagerly his arrival to make the flush.

Three species of western hill-country game birds can also fly with the same explosive acceleration as the prey group just described. Accipiters, wild or trained, also avidly pursue these birds; however, they are a much more difficult flight, if not for the hawk, then certainly for the huntsman. The reason for this difficulty is the kind of terrain these species inhabit. The species referred to are introduced chukar partridge, native western blue-grouse and mountain quail. When they are moving about on foot, or when they are feeding, these birds slowly work their way uphill. Once they are startled, these birds flush straight out from the hillside and then scale off downslope at high speed. When they are flushed from high ridges or from mountainsides, they may drop for vertical distances of 500 to 1,000 feet (150 to 300 meters) or more. This occurrence is of no consequence at all to a pursuing raptor, but obviously no earthbound falconer can follow such a flight.

While these species can be taken with trained accipiters, they must be sought in as gentle, cliff-free terrain as they inhabit. If these species are flushed when they are only a few yards above a valley floor while they are closely pursued, they are then forced to exert themselves and they must, therefore, soon seek cover. If they are forced to flush a second time, they can cope no better than do pheasant, quail or woodland grouse. Nevertheless, except for flights to poults or to the occasional individual first flushed on the level, flights to these hill grouse and partridge average about double the distances of flights to flatland species.

The grouse of deserts, grasslands and tundras — in North America, these birds are sage, sharp-tailed and pinnated grouse and the ptarmigans — are different from the former group because they have rich, red breast musculature which is well supplied with blood and with oxygen. While these species are not the equal of the former group in the rapidity of their initial acceleration, they, nevertheless, attain higher sustained speeds of much longer duration. Wild goshawks also hunt these prey species, but with considerably less success. As a group, these birds are much more subject to predation from falcons than they are from accipiters. Only goshawks can capture the adults of these grouse and then only if the halsband is used and the hawk is worked in conjunction with pointing dogs because the birds must be taken as they first rise or not at all. They readily distance any goshawk once they attain their full flying speed and they do not easily tire.

While the traditional, and still the usual, method of hunting with an accipiter is to walk about with a bird perched and unhooded on the glove, contemporary falconers have contributed some new ways of bringing their hawks within range of some quarries previously considered impossible. It is ridiculous for a man on foot, if he is carrying a hawk, to attempt to get anywhere near crows, but it is not at all difficult to approach them closely if a person rather slowly drives an automobile along earth or gravel secondary roads in farming areas. A goshawk or a Harris's hawk suddenly darting out of the side window of such an automobile while the vehicle is still in motion always catches crows completely off-guard. Magpies or starlings can be similarly surprised and Cooper's hawks or sharp-shins can take them exactly the same way. Cold weather, midwinter hunting of these quarries, as well as of pheasants, gray partridge, rabbits or hares, can be both comfortable and successful when accipiters are given this kind of opportunity.

Perhaps the most unorthodox and the most imaginative of the new techniques of taking game with accipiters and with Harris's hawks is the one devised by western American falconers, who take their birds in vehicles along secondary roads at night and fly them straight down the headlight beams to nocturnal mammals.

Whenever an accipiter repeatedly and successfully takes game in the same hunting area, it quickly learns to recognize the places where game is most likely to appear. This recognition develops because they remember both the location and the circumstances of any previous success. This repetition, if it is long continued, develops a highly-specialized hawk, one which takes a narrow range of quarry with absolute certainty when it does fly, but one which also becomes so critical and so discerning of the pre-conditions to success it is unlikely to fly at all unless these preconditions are met. These characteristics are the behavioral fixations of old hawks; they are the accumulated result of years of repetitive successes and equally repetitive failures. Accipiters are most exciting, but least successful, in their first year because during this time they try for anything. Cooper's hawks reach their highest capability from about their third to their fifth year while goshawks reach their prime from their third to about their tenth year. Sharp-shinned hawks seldom live much more than four years, but if they live to their second or third season they become extremely efficient little hawks, especially if they have been permitted to specialize.

Every derogatory word in the English language could aptly be used to describe the inner nature of accipiters. They are mean, cunning, sneaky, vicious, devious, sulky, unforgiving, vengeful and malicious. Unless they are taken young and so imprinted to man, they develop no attachment to their trainer. Foolish is the falconer who permits himself to become attached to one of these hawks because they remain loners even after years of close association and after hundreds of successful hunts. They forever view their trainer and everything else with such suspicion that the least suspected provocation may take either the form of overt glaring malice or crazed, wild-eyed fright. They are surely not every man's hawk, but whatever their behavior accipiters are never boring.

Falcons

Most of the problems encountered when flying falcons are a direct result of their excellence. However, the flights with falcons differ from those of other species because the simplest flights are the most difficult for the falconer; it is because of this difference that its more advanced and more complex flights have been developed — primarily as a means of keeping the action within the range of human capability to follow.

All gyrfalcons, some peregrines and the occasional prairie falcon are capable of overtaking, in level flight and with no advantage of surprise, the open-country grouse and the ptarmigan as well as swift and enduring species such as the Wilson's snipe, shorebirds and waterfowl. Wild falcons regularly accomplish this feat; however, no experienced falconer deliberately seeks such flights. When they do inadvertently occur, he fervently hopes his falcon will fail. The reason is simple. In this kind of chase, the successful falcon is also a lost falcon.

The reasons for this result require explanation. To begin with, because falcons normally hunt in flight, they tend to become impatient when they are carried about unhooded. This impatience leads to repeated bating and, except for only the merlin and the kestrel, they must be flown "out of the hood" or on direct pursuit flights. For these flights, they are unhooded after their quarry has been flushed. This action of unhooding, no matter how skilled and how dexterous, causes a delay which gives any quarry capable of rapid acceleration a considerable lead. Falcons do not have rapid aerial acceleration themselves and it follows if the pursuit is to such species as a sharp-tailed grouse or a mallard, the falcon, already delayed, will continue to lose distance. Thus, by the time the falcon reaches the flight speed of its quarry, the flight will have already covered a lineal distance approaching a quarter mile during that thirty-second interval. By this time, both birds will be moving at speeds in the forty miles-per-hour range and they are usually going straight away from the falconer. Thirty seconds later they are out of the range of unaided human vision. From this time onward, the falconer has no idea either where or how far to go or how the flight ended. The best he can hope for is the quarry somehow distanced or somehow eluded his falcon, in which case persistent luring in the direction the flight took will probably result in recovery. Otherwise, if the falcon has killed the quarry, recovery is unlikely. The falcon will pluck and will eat to repletion and then will seek a secluded, comfortable perch for a time interval of some eight to twelve hours. Following this period of rest, the falcon will again be interested in a lure and may even look for the falconer in the area where the flight began, if it is in familiar terrain. Otherwise, unless it is carrying a radio transmitter, the bird is lost.

Even the mounted falconers of unfenced steppe and desert areas avoided such flights. Nevertheless, it might be pointed out there is a great difference in the probable outcome of a horseman casting a falcon off downslope as he rides at full speed in order to flush out a group of waterfowl on a little pond ahead of the falcon, and of a footman casting off the same kind of falcon under identical conditions.

UPLAND GAME BIRDS
Wherever the landscape is open enough to permit falcons to be

flown in direct pursuit of the white-fleshed upland game birds, the results can be worthwhile because, despite the high initial acceleration of their quarry, falcons are always capable of either overtaking these birds or of forcing them to seek cover. In either case, the flight, even to pheasant (unless downhill), seldom covers a distance greater than half a mile. When these quarries reach cover ahead of their pursuer, most falcons, even the impatient gyrfalcon, will tower aloft to lose speed, then slowly circle above the place where their quarry disappeared. This practice is the falconine counterpart of the perched goshawk waiting at mark and it is, of course, "waiting on," however briefly the falcon may hold this position. If, when this situation occurs, the falconer (and his dog) can come up and can reflush quickly enough to result in a stoop-kill while the falcon is still in position, the length of time the falcon subsequently holds position will each time be more prolonged. Thus, it is worth carrying a live substitute quarry for this purpose. Without a dog, it is often impossible for a man to find these crouched or hidden birds because, just as when accipiters hard-fly them, they often refuse to fly a second time. Needless to say, when either the dog or the huntsman takes quarries in cover, they should be immediately served to the falcon.

Direct flights to these same quarries are also rewarding when they are initiated from inside a slowly-moving vehicle because in such a vehicle the falcon, upon being unhooded, can immediately see while remaining unseen. Such flights do not significantly differ from those already described, but here again it is the falconer who must discriminate between the white-fleshed and the dark-fleshed quarries because his falcon will not. When they are seen feeding out in a snow-covered stubblefield, there is little difference in the appearance of a covey of gray partridge and a covey of sharp-tailed grouse. To the novice, it would appear the falcon would have about the same chance of success with the one as with the other. However, the flight to the partridge has a high chance of success with a low risk of loss while the flight to the grouse has a low chance of success with a high risk of loss.

FLOCK QUARRIES

Intermediate between the direct fast pursuits of the short-winged upland game birds and the high, ringing flights are the pursuits of certain flocking species which are capable of strong and erratic flight, but of only moderate speed. Starlings and blackbirds are the best examples of this group, although crows probably belong here rather than in the next group. These species tend to frequent open country and they react with two separate and definite defences when falcons attack. One of these defences is to seek refuge in brush, trees, canes, reeds or standing crops. Secondly, if they are forced into the air from such refuge, or if they are caught out in open fields away from such refuge, they will take wing in a dense, compact flock. The tactic here is to confuse the falcon through flock maneuvering and to prevent the falcon from selecting any one bird. The ensuing flights are interesting and exciting. The flock under attack maneuvers like a shoal of herring, twisting and turning, breaking apart to let the falcon pass through and then reforming. Most falcons, even gyrfalcons, chase these flocks with marked enthusiasm. Success is not high and it more likely goes to the smaller falcons. Merlins are excellent for these flights while the little tiercels of the arctic peregrine and the tiercel prairie falcons closely follow. Although aerial distances covered in such pursuits may be high, the flight changes direction so frequently ground distances are low; in relatively still air, a man on foot can easily follow the flight. The direct pursuit of wild falcons after shorebirds falls under this type of flight, but the higher flight speed of shorebirds and their tendency to move in one direction largely precludes them as practical quarry for trained falcons.

The flight to crows usually has some of the characteristics of these flock pursuits, but where the flight is initiated to a single crow or when the attacking falcon succeeds in cutting one crow out of the flock for individual pursuit, what follows takes on some of the characteristics of the ringing flights.

RINGING FLIGHTS

When a short-eared owl is flushed from the grass and takes off in slow, wavering flight ahead of a goshawk, it is usually captured within somewhat less than six yards from the point it left the ground. That such a bird should be able to test the stamina and the flying skills of the finest falcon may seem puzzling and contradictory, however, such is the case. When a falcon, be it gyrfalcon, peregrine or prairie, is unhooded and is released behind this slow-flying owl, the immediate impression of any uninitiated observer is the owl will quickly be captured because on this initial tailchase the falcon closes the gap at double or at triple the owl's speed. Then, just as the falcon drops its feet for the strike, the owl vanishes. The falconer, if not always the falcon, can see what has happened and how amazing it is. In the final split-second, the owl has abruptly flipped either over or under the falcon and reversed its direction of flight. The owl begins to climb skyward the moment it completes the maneuver. Being large of wing and light of body, it can almost vertically rise skyward. In the meantime, the weight and the speed of the falcon carries it far out in a curving outrun and when it glances back it will see the owl already above it.

The next round, if the falcon is strong and if it is determined, introduces the classic ringing flight, the flight the ancients loved and extolled above all others. It is an upward-moving contest of aerial skills and an exciting demonstration of some of the fundamental laws of aerodynamics. In this contest, the falcon, because of its heavier wing-loading, must orbit its slower-moving competitor at high speed, striving in this way to spiral above the competitor from which position the falcon can then aim a short stoop nearly straight down. This stoop is not so easy to dodge, but if it is dodged, the result is loss of height and of further spiraling. Although many flights end in failure, most females of any of the large falcons show great tenacity and great determination while many tiercels can hardly be persuaded to persevere at all following the failure of the initial strike. There is no doubt the preference for the falcon proper, which is so much a part of the classic literature, had its origin in these flights and in the much-higher willingness of the females to persevere in their efforts to capture and to kill the big-winged birds. Many diverse species have been selected as quarries for these flights over the centuries, all of which react in the same, or a similar, way when a falcon attacks. Amongst these quarries are bustards, cranes, herons, harriers, buzzards, kites, gulls, rooks, crows and owls. Some of these quarries are predators and their presence on this list may be significant because of all of these quarries, falcons only regularly kill some of the smaller bustards and some of the smaller gulls for food. Some of the others are amongst the kind of big-winged birds which most alarm and most infuriate breeding falcons, especially the females. This fact suggests the link to all of them, as quarry, lies here because they appear to be pursued and to be killed much more from hatred than from hunger.

Except in windy weather, these high flights are not difficult to follow unless they go so high as to take both birds out of sight. At any rate, both birds tend to drift downwind at approximately the speed of the wind. Kills sometime take place high in the air with both birds then slowly falling together. Less frequently, a grazing strike may disable the quarry and send it spinning downward. The quarry is then followed down and it is killed outright with a much harder strike delivered at the limit of a long, steep stoop as it falls. For large and dangerous quarries such as cranes or kites, two falcons were often trained to fly together. These falcons were not true pairs of male and female; instead, they were always two females. Wolf's famous painting of a gray gyrfalcon and a white gyrfalcon locked in combat with a red kite accurately depicts the termination of this kind of flight.

Disregarding any contemporary interpretations of the legality or otherwise of flying falcons to some of these quarries, one finds no lack of material for these flights with gyrfalcons, peregrines or prairie falcons on this continent. Sandhill cranes and Swainson's hawks are adequate American equivalents of the Eurasian cranes and buzzards while herons, gulls, short-eared owls and harriers are common to both and they are as abundant in contemporary North America as they ever were in historic Eurasia. North America has no kites comparable to the red kite, or the rooks, but North America does have plenty of crows.

GAME-HAWKING

The anticipatory or the waiting-on flights have not inappropriately become known in North America under the term "game hawking." As already pointed out, the technique was developed in western Europe during the decline of falconry as a means of permitting the unhorsed falconer to continue to fly falcons. In practice, these flights subdivide into two distinct categories: those to upland game and those to waterfowl. Of these flights, the flight to waterfowl is the less complex, although not necessarily the more successful.

The really significant difference in the two types of quarry is shown when the falcon is flown to waterfowl; the falcon will almost immediately see its quarry after being unhooded, whereas on the flight to upland game, the quarry will remain unseen for a considerable period of time after the falcon is in the air. This apparent minor difference is of major significance because gyrfalcons, many prairie falcons and even some peregrines which are impossible or which are difficult to persuade to wait on when no quarry is in sight are willing to hold steadily over quarry which they can see. Waterfowl flights, therefore, require less highly-specialized (or trained) birds than are required for most upland game. Finally, with waterfowl as quarry, the use of dogs is not mandatory as is so often the case with upland game. Dogs can be an asset in flushing if they are under control, but they are not really needed.

WATERFOWL

The only group of waterfowl which provide consistent flights for falcons are pond or puddle ducks, mallards, pintails, gadwalls, widgeons, shovellers and teals. The falconer who seeks these quarries will sometimes find his falcon has taken a coot or one of the diving ducks. These latter species, when singly occurring or when in minor groups in the company of the easily-flushed puddle ducks, are inclined to flush along with them. When these species are flushed, they are exceedingly vulnerable and the falcon is liable to deliberately select them. Otherwise, they usually inhabit water areas too large for falconry. Bufflehead, scaup, ring-necked duck and sometimes goldeneye occasionally frequent small ponds. Of these species, only scaup and ringneck can sometimes be flushed clear. Goldeneye and bufflehead can be infuriating when a falcon is over them. They will fly only from end to end of even the smallest pond and they will draw stoop after stoop while going back headlong into the water ahead of the falcon each time; they always refuse to clear the water and to go out over land.

Waterfowl sometimes occur in situations where the novice would believe a falcon could not miss, but where, in fact, the capture of a duck is much more difficult than it appears; the falcon is likely to be lost if a flight is attempted. Chief amongst these situations are the conditions which occur when ducks are feeding in great numbers, whether they be in dry grainfields during autumn, in shallow water mudfields or in estuarine areas. A falcon released near or released amidst great numbers of ducks causes those nearest it to rise. In doing so, they provoke an immediate attack from the falcon. The result is instant confusion for both the falcon and the falconer. The presence nearby of so many ducks prevents the falcon from singling out any one bird while the falconer cannot distinguish his falcon nor hear its bells amidst the wavering roar of wings. In such a situation, there is neither the chance nor the tendency for the falcon to climb up against the sky. New ducks flushing ahead draw the falcon ever onward or to this side and to that side. Sometimes, a quick opportunistic snatch amidst the confusion results in success and the falcon is suddenly down with its duck. However, the chances of the falconer discerning this success are almost nil. With the falcon either no longer flying or no longer near the falconer, the hordes of ducks again begin to settle. Out there somewhere amongst all those waterfowl there might be a falcon down with one of them. If so, where? And if not, where has the falcon gone? To go out in the water swinging a lure is obviously ridiculous; with so many quarry about, what falcon will come to the lure? Listening for the bells is also useless. Locating a falcon, even one down with a duck on dry, firm, terrain, in such a situation is almost impossible. If this foolish flight has been attempted over wet or over muddy terrain, attempts to locate the falcon will be hopeless. In falconry, there can actually be too much quarry; great flocks of thousands of ducks well away from extensive water are only a trap for the in-experienced falconer.

When waterfowl are located in natural meandering creeks, they can be taken. However, it is difficult for falcons to capture waterfowl in artificially-straightened creeks or in drainage ditches because it is nearly impossible for the falconer to move the quarries out over land once they become aware of the falcon. They can be flushed readily enough and in flushing they may well draw a stoop from the falcon, but they will fly straight along the ditch, keeping water under them all the time as they are ready to crash back into the water if a stoop comes close. Flights along such ditches are all too often abortive and useless as they end in failure for the falcon and in exhaustion for the falconer.

The really exciting and the really successful flights to waterfowl occur when small to medium-sized flocks, from singles or pairs up to over fifty together, are found in a series of small ponds a quarter-mile or more apart or in the widened areas of a slow, meandering creek. Under these conditions, predictable flights with a low risk of loss are the rule.

Assuming the falconer has familiarized himself beforehand with the location and the size of a pond and any others nearby, the procedure is simple. The pond is usually checked from a distance to ascertain quarry is present. If so, the hooded falcon is then brought as close to the quarry as the terrain will permit. If the pond is fringed with vegetation or if it is an artificial impoundment, it can sometimes be closely approached from concealment and the falcon unhooded and cast out over the ducks while the falconer is still hidden only a scant thirty yards or so away. At the other extreme, if the pond is a natural pothole in prairie grassland or if it lies at the bottom of a sageland basin, the falcon may have to be released from a distance of a quarter-mile or even more. In any case, the appearance of the falcon alone with no interference from the falconer is not a cause for concern or for alarm to ducks on the water. On coming over the pond, the falcon may begin stooping at the ducks. Inexperienced birds may continue this stooping until the falconer comes up to make the flush. Such falcons have no significant height advantage to convert into speed and they are not really "waiting on." However, if the falconer is careful and if he can time his final rush to the exact moment when the falcon, after climbing up on an outrun from one pass, has turned back or is beginning to turn back, his falcon may take out a duck just beyond the point at which it has cleared the edge of the pond. Even some experienced falcons almost always make a few such passes before they climb well over the ducks; others go over them just once, low and fast, before they continue on at high speed and return in a wide arc in order to come back at a commanding height. In any case, the experienced falcons orient at once to the ducks and go well above them to await the arrival of the falconer. For the flush to be successful, much depends on the component species of the waterfowl flock and the experience, the species and even the sex of the falcon as related to the size and the kind of quarry.

Gyrfalcons of either sex and some female peregrines, but only the occasional prairie falcon, can manage mallards. Pintails, gadwalls, and widgeons can be regularly taken with either peregrine or prairie falcons, but not with some tiercels. Some peregrine tiercels will handle widgeons, but the ducks for tiercels are shovellers and teal. In all flights to waterfowl, there is a real advantage in flying a large falcon because waterfowl often occur in mixed flocks. A gyrfalcon will usually take something from almost any flock, ranging from a great, heavy canvasback down to the tiniest greenwing teal; if mallards only are flushed under a prairie tiercel, it is not likely to do much.

When ponds are in a series and they are not a great distance apart, the risk of losing the falcon is greatly reduced. Gyrfalcons, in particular, are regularly swift, persistent and often successful in tailchases; however, any falcon which has made solid contact with a duck, but has not felled it, will pursue the duck with great determination or sometimes, in error, a different one which has not been touched. Bodies of water nearby determine both the direction and the ultimate distance of any such flight because the duck, if it is hard-pressed, will go straight for the nearest body of water. The flight will terminate either there, with the duck safe and the falcon looking for a lure, or somewhere along a straight line between the two bodies of water, with the duck taken and the falcon down with it and fairly easy to locate. This type of incident is why totally isolated, small ponds, however attractive to waterfowl and however tempting to the falconer, result in high-hazard flights.

UPLAND GAME

Flights to upland game require the falcon to go aloft above the falconer with no quarry in sight and hold this position for varying periods of time as an act of trust or of faith. This practice is based on the prior experience that the falconer will ultimately produce quarry. This type of falconry is more specialized and more demanding than the flights to waterfowl, although they are not necessarily any more exciting or any more rewarding. The ever-present imperative in upland game-hawking is the falconer seldom or, if possible, never fail to serve his falcon. Therefore, it is of paramount importance the falconer not only know with absolute certainty game is present, but also its exact whereabouts before the falcon is released.

The red grouse of the highlands of Scotland has long been considered a classic quarry for the peregrine. The procedures followed in the flight to this species could well be considered a model for successful upland game-hawking anywhere. The red grouse is a rather large, strong-flying game bird of open heather-lands. It is actually a ptarmigan *(lagopus)* which is one of the dark-fleshed species which can fly far and fly fast without tiring. Being a ptarmigan, it is a social species which occurs in coveys numbering from five to a dozen individuals. These coveys tend to crouch and to hide at the approach of any large predator; then they explode into simultaneous flight. They are, therefore, said to "hold well" to pointing dogs. Since the red grouse is a hill species, using dogs to locate a covey does not necessarily mean a flight will be risked, although the initial search is, of course, conducted in reasonably favorable terrain. Only when a covey is located in what the falconer deems to be a flyable situation, and with the dogs holding on point, is the falcon unhooded and cast into the wind. Now, although the falcon cannot and will not see the grouse until they are flushed, the grouse will immediately see the falcon against the sky and they will prefer not to flush as long as the falcon is within their field of vision. This reluctance on the part of the grouse means once the falcon is flying, the falconer is in control of both the timing and the direction of the imminent flight. He can make due allowances for the direction and the velocity of the wind, combined with other variables such as the direction and the distance of hills, gullies or thickets. In theory, if not always in practice, the falconer will wait until the falcon stops working on its upward climb and begins to coast and to sail. He then moves around the dogs to a position upwind of the grouse and he delays until the falcon has also come upwind of them and it is just beginning to turn back downwind. At that instant, the dogs are signalled and the falconer and the dogs rush forward to flush the grouse.

The theoretical result is for the falcon to make an immediate headlong, downwind stoop as the grouse break clear of the heather, culminating in a resounding thump and a cloud of feathers as one of them is hit hard and is sent tumbling back to the ground. The falcon rebounds skyward, glances back over its wings to mark the falling grouse, stalls out, turns into the wind to drop lightly down on its prey and completes the kill with a bite through the neck. After the killing is complete, the falcon will begin an unconcerned leisurely plucking of the dead grouse as the falconer, his assistants and his dogs make their way to the spot.

Not all flights to upland game, not even those to red grouse and to gray partridge which are amongst the most predictable quarries, have such a predictable outcome. Of the native North American upland game bird species, only willow ptarmigan closely match red grouse in size and in behavior. However, the range of this species is too far north for it to have received any significant attention from North American falconers. The introduced European gray partridge, however, is widely available across the northern United States and across southern Canada. Most British falconers consider red grouse generally to be above the size capability of peregrine tiercels and barely within the capability of most females. As two of the three mid-latitude North American grassland grouse are somewhat larger, and the third species is much larger, than the red grouse, it is not surprising they have proven exceedingly difficult quarries for North American falconers flying peregrines or prairie falcons. Pinnated grouse, the "prairie chickens" of the long-grass prairies of the midwest, have so far received little attention, but the sharp-tailed grouse, the "prairie chickens" of the short-grass plains and the aspen parklands, together with the big sage grouse have been well tested. Of the two, the sharp-tails are easily the better quarry for falcons because they are a much smaller species and the coveys hold well to dogs. However, they are considerably larger than the red grouse and, as already noted, they are both swift and enduring in flight. Sharp-tails usually distance anything except a gyrfalcon if they are not hit hard on the first or the second stoop. Sage grouse are not as swift, but they are just as enduring. They are the most difficult of the grassland grouse to approach and they are the least inclined to lie to dogs. The coveys will, however, sometimes crouch when they see a falcon against the sky. Since they are a rather visible species for grouse, they can sometimes be brought fairly close under a falcon without any use of dogs if the falcon is simply cast into the air when a group of grouse is seen; afterwards, if their position has been carefully marked, they can be flushed out under the falcon in the usual way.

PHEASANT

The big, colorful, introduced ring-neck pheasant, although certainly the quarry on which North American falconers have focussed more time and more energy than any other, remains, like sage grouse, ever difficult and ever unrewarding. This species is really too large for any falcon smaller than the gyrfalcon. The tendency it has to run ahead of dogs and to flush "wild" is notorious; if this tendency is annoying for the gunner, it is doubly so for the falconer. In practice, it is nearly impossible to make pheasant flush at the optimal moment for the falcon. Even when the best of field-dogs point it out, the pheasant will manage to creep a few yards away from where the dog holds point after espying a falcon aloft. By not being exactly where the dog indicates, the pheasant is able to delay being flushed until the dreaded falcon is out of position downwind. This strategy helps the pheasant to time its own escape upwind, usually in a dash to dense cover and to safety.

OTHER GAME BIRDS

The introduced western hill-partridge, the chukar, although easily within the size range of either prairie falcon or peregrine, is not ideal quarry largely because of its pheasant-like tendency to run ahead of dogs; this tendency makes the partridge hard to pin down for a predictable flush. Where this partridge can be located on sloping, rather than precipitous, terrain, direct downslope pursuit can more effectively take it than any other pursuit method.

Generally, the smaller species of native North American upland game are better quarries for falcons than the larger kinds. The eastern bobwhite quail, a level-country, covey species found in field edges and in low brush which holds well to dogs, has long been a prized game bird for gunners and is as perfect a species for game-hawking as can be found anywhere. It is large enough for peregrine falcons, but it is also small enough to be within the size range of even the smallest prairie tiercels. The several varieties of the western valley quail are a bit more like chukars in running before dogs. They are also far more difficult than bobwhite to flush out across clear open areas.

OTHER QUARRY

In North America, there are three remaining species which behave in ways which make them excellent quarries for falcons, even though they cannot be properly classified as upland game. Two of them provide merely interesting flights, but the third provides, at its best, the fastest and the most spectacular flight in North American game-hawking. These species are the meadowlark, the Wilson's snipe and the mourning dove. All three are singularly attractive to falcons and the flush of any of them under a high-flying falcon will always result in the most reckless headlong stoop.

Although in no way related to any game bird species and never given game bird status, meadowlarks have, nevertheless, developed many of the characteristics of the grassland game birds and they are the primary prey species of many pairs of wild prairie falcons. Just what a falconer walking about in grasslands under a falcon is "hunting," or what his "intent" may be, particularly when that grassland may be frequented by chukar partridge, might be legally difficult to define. It is even more difficult to define the intentions of a falcon. Be that as it may, the fact is anyone randomly wandering anywhere in the western grasslands more or less constantly flushes meadowlarks. They rise from the grass like little partridges to fly a few yards before again settling in the grass. When a falcon is in the air, however, few if any meadowlarks will be found. However, if a falcon is carried hooded, the larks will flush out as usual. If the falcon is unhooded and cast off just as a lark flushes, the lark will drop, chattering in alarm, back into the grass almost the moment the falcon is airborne; the falcon will immediately fly over to the spot where the lark disappeared and circle, or even expectantly hover, although usually at no great height. While it is almost impossible for a man to reflush the hidden meadowlark, one does not need a highly-bred pointer to find it and to nose it out. Almost any dog can carry out this purpose for the falconer.

Meadowlarks are not swift, nor are they artful masters of the aerial dodge and the turn. Their one chance of escape is to get back into the grass as quickly as possible. Even from a low pitch, the falcon usually has time for only one quick stoop before the lark vanishes and the entire sequence must be repeated. Lark flights are by no means great flights, but they can be exciting and they require less perfection on the part of the falcon, the falconer and the dog than any other kind of flight to upland game. These meadowlarks are, therefore, perhaps the least difficult of North American game-hawking quarries, but they are surely the ideal wild quarry for a novice flying a first-year eyess of either a peregrine falcon or a prairie falcon, particularly if it is a tiercel of the latter species.

Wilson's snipes inhabit open wet meadows. Wilson's snipes tend to be sporadic in their appearance, but when they do become abundant, they are well worth brief attention from any falconer with a good falcon. When Wilson's snipes are abundant, they are usually sufficiently well dispersed so random walking will regularly flush only single individuals. They are one of the few species which provide superb flights when they are hunted in a random and a speculative way with the falcon aloft. Wilson's snipes evade well and they are seldom taken on the first stoop. Flights often degenerate into the tailchase; the snipe is sometimes outflown and it is driven back to shelter in ground cover, but even when this occurrence happens, the pursuit is so erratic no significant lineal distance is covered. Either sex of peregrines so avidly pursue snipes no amount of failure appears to dampen their willingness to chase this species. Kills are rare, but the flights are superb.

Mourning doves are quarries different from either Wilson's snipes or from meadowlarks. This species is one which, at its best, can provide the most spectacular and the most dramatic of all North American game flights. Mourning doves are a common, widely-distributed species over most of mid-latitude North America. They are exceedingly swift in straightaway flight, so swift they can regularly outdistance most falcons. Indeed, outdistancing falcons is their normal escape procedure when they are under attack. Doves inhabit, by preference, open or semi-open landscapes, move about in small flocks and, despite their rather small size, they are highly visible. They can be readily located without the use of dogs either through watching where flocks are alighting to feed or through watching where they are seeking water. In either case, if doves are on the ground when they see a falcon in the air, they crouch and they hold. If they are carefully marked, they can be easily flushed with no help from dogs, even with a falcon high above and obvious; they then fly straightaway at tremendous speed. Mourning doves must be taken from aloft or not at all, but their headlong speed and straight-line flight combine to bring falcons down with their utmost velocity. Peregrines, particularly the tiercels, soon learn to attain great heights when they are regularly flown to this quarry; some of them go so high they are completely out of sight. From this position, they come down in single hurtling dives in what are without doubt the most spectacular stoops in falconry. Dove falcons are specialists, but mourning doves are sufficiently common and sufficiently available to be well worth this special training because any falcon which will fly pigeons will also fly doves. Therefore, the training of a dove falcon is not difficult.

In many ways, the falcons combine most of the best characteristics of all other hawks of the chase. Generally speaking, it could be said they have the cool unconcern for distractions of a red-tail, an attachment to their trainer equal with, if not higher than, a Harris's hawk, the disdain for distance of an eagle and the enthusiasm for hunting of a goshawk. All these characteristics combine with a superiority of structure and of design which gives them a capability of higher speed and greater endurance than any of the others. In their attitude toward their trainer, they tend to be forbearing and forgiving, suffering minor indignities without rancor or fear. In their own distinctive way, they are among the most beautiful of birds, tight-plumaged and trim. Falcons also have about them a kind of cool, dignified and almost-arrogant presence in repose which sets them apart even from the great eagles.

Suggested Readings

The literature pertaining to birds of prey has become so extensive in the last two decades that the mere listing of titles and authors would require a volume larger than this entire book. The scientific literature is scattered in a multitude of scientific and ornithological journals and university papers. The falconry literature, while just as voluminous, tends to be more concentrated and therefore more readily available in the two English-language falconry club journals and publications—the North American Falconers' Association and the British Falconers' club.

The following list includes English-language books only. In addition to falconry and hawking titles, some major hardcover publications are included. Many of the books listed here contain biographies that list further titles that are not listed here.

Beebe, Frank Lyman. 1976. *Hawks, Falcons and Falconry*. Published by Hancock House, Saanichton, Seattle, Buffalo. 320 pp. Updated version of North American Falconry and Hunting Hawks. Species accounts are from "Field Studies of the Falconiformes of British Columbia."

Beebe, Frank Lyman, and Harold Melvin Webster. 1964. *North American Falconry and Hunting Hawks*. Privately published, Denver. xii–315 pp. The first illustrated text on the techniques of training hawks and falcons to be published in North America. The knowledge and practical experience has been updated in The Compleat Falconer.

Bent, A. C. 1937. *Life Histories of North American Birds of Prey* (Order Falconiformes—Part 1). U.S. National Museum Bulletin 167, Washington, D.C., 409 pp.

Bosakowski, Thomas. 1999. *The Northern Goshawk: Ecology, Behavior, and Management in North America*. Published by Hancock House Publishers, Surrey, Blaine, 80 pp. A scientific look at the northern goshawk.

Brown, L. and D. Amadon. 1968. *Eagles, Hawks and Falcons of the World*, Parts 1 and 2. Published by McGraw-Hill, New York, 945 pp. The best all-purpose reference on world-wide birds of prey.

Burnham, W. 1997. *A Fascination with Falcons*. Published by Hancock House Publishers, Surrey, Blaine, 234 pp. An autobiographical account of a biologist's adventures following falcons from Greenland to the Tropics.

Cade, T. J. 1982. *The Falcons of the World*. Published by Cornell University Press. 188 pp. The equivalent on falcons to Brown and Amadon's world birds of prey, but updated with some new information. All species are illustrated in color by David R. Digby.

Cade, T. J. et al. 1988. *Peregrine Falcon Populations*. Published by The Peregrine Fund, Boise, Id. This is the proceedings of the 1985 peregrine conference in Madison, Wisconsin.

Craighead, F., and J. Craighead. 1956. *Hawks, Owls and Wildlife*. Published by Stackpole, Harrisburg, Pa., 443 pp.

Dekker, Dick. 1999. *Bolt from the Blue*. Published by Hancock House Publishers, Surrey, Blaine, 192 pp. An anecdotal book about peregrine falcons.

Fox, Nick. 1995. *Understanding the Bird of Prey*. Published by Hancock House Publishers, Surrey, Blaine, 376. A comprehensive and masterfully written gathering of data on birds of prey.

Frank, Saul. 1994. *City Peregrine: A Ten-year Saga of New York City Falcons*. Published by Hancock House Publishers, Surrey, Blaine, 313 pp. The captivating story of peregrines living and breeding in New York City.

Grossman, M. L., and J. Hamlet. 1964. *Birds of Prey of the World*. Published by Clarkson N. Potter, Inc. New York, 496 pp. Not as well written, organized or detailed as Brown and Amadon's two-volume work, but first photographs ever published of many species; owls are included.

Haak, Bruce. 1992. *The Hunting Falcon*. Published by Hancock House Publishers, Surrey, Blaine, 239 pp. A fresh approach to the sport of falconry.

Haak, Bruce. 1995. *Pirate of the Plains*. Published by Hancock House Publishers, Surrey, Blaine, 208 pp. An autobiographical account of research on the prairie falcon.

Harting, J. E. 1884. *Hints on the Management of Hawks*. The Field Office, London. 84 pp. Second Edition 1898 268 pp. Especially good section (second edition) on methods of capturing passage falcons.

Hickey, J. J., Editor. 1969. *Peregrine Falcon Populations: Their Biology and Decline*. University of Wisconsin Press. Madison. 650 pp. This book is a compilation of papers presented at the "world" conference on peregrines in Madison 1965. The conclusions reached by Hickey are in disagreement with many of the papers presented at the conference, but they nevertheless led to the official "endangered" status of peregrine falcons (and gyrfalcons too) in 1971.

Hollinshead, M. 1995. *Hawking with Golden Eagles.* Published by Hancock House Publishers, Surrey, Blaine, 173 pp. An autobiographical account of the sport of hawking with golden eagles.

Illingworth, Frank. 1947. *Falcons and Falconry.* Published by Blandford Press, London. 11 pp. Anecdotal treatment of British Falconry.

Kotsiopoulos, George. 1999. *Falconry Uncommon.* Published by Hancock House Publishers, Surrey, Blaine, 120 pp. A collection of classic treatises about the art and sport of falconry.

Latham Symon. 1615. *Falconry or the Falcons' Lure and Cure.* Published by Roger Jackson, London. Two books, 150 and 148 pp. respectively. A classic early publication with many editions and a contemporary reprinting.

Mavrogordato, J. G. 1960. *A Hawk for the Bush.* Published by H. F. And G. Witherby, London. 144 pp. A remarkable contemporary classic on the training of accipiters.

Michell, E. B. 1900. *The Art and Practice of Hawking.* Published by Methuen and Co. London. 291 pp. Prior to 1961, this was the definitive work on falconry in English.

Stevens, R. 1956. *Observations on Modern Falconry.* Privately published, Shrewsbury. 112 pp. Excellent insight combined with completely contemporary and rational approach, entirely about falcons.

Stevens, R. 1975. *Laggard.* Falconiforme Press Ltd. Saskatoon, Canada. 310 pp. Beautifully written account of hawking in Ireland with peregrines and gyrfalcons.

Stevens, R. *The Taming of Genghis.* 127 pp. A well-written account of a first experience in training a goshawk.

Stevens, R. 1995. *A Life with Birds.* Published by Hancock House Publishers, Surrey, Blaine, 156 pp. An autobiographical account of a life spent with birds of prey.

White, T. H. 1964. *The Goshawk.* Published by G. P. Putnam's Sons, London. 215 pp. Superb writing of a first experience in training a goshawk.

Wood, Casey A., and F. Majorie Fyfe. 1943. *The Art of Falconry (De arte venandi cum avibus) of Frederick II of Hohenstaufen.* Stanford University Press, Stanford University. 637 pp. Often described as "the first modern man" Frederick II was far ahead of his time in analytical thinking. The book is almost entirely about gyrfalcons and includes an extensive bibliography.

INDEX

Accipiters..................... 12,47,48,172
Accipiters, training 144-147
Aplomado falcon 25,29
Arctic Peregrine 182
Aspergillosis 149
Assateague Island 112
Audubon.............................89
Automobile Hunting.............. 178,179

Bating 141
Beak 136
Bell(s) 95,97,98
Birds of prey historically.............. 83-91
Brancher(s) 111
Broun, Maurice 87
Buteos 12,47

Calling off 158
Cape May 87
Casting 130
Chukar 159,162
Cooper's Hawk..................... 63-65
Cope(ing) 136
Cornell University 14,92
Creance 140,141

DDT 92
Disease...............................149
Dogs 138,161
Dove, Mourning 162,190-193
Duluth 112

Eagle 169
Eagle, bald 84
Endangered species....................92
Entering 141,142,159
Excretions 130
Extinction........................ 14,16
Eyess 123,124,125,126,127,130,131

Falcon(s)............. 9,10,11,12,13,150,179
Falcon, Haggard 123
Falcons, forest........................12
Falconers 12
Falconry 12
Falconry, future of 16,111
Falconry, history of 60,85,150
Falconry, North American 12,16,134
Falconry, as recreation 89
Feathers 132,133
Feeding 129,130,131,139
Ferruginous Hawk 73-76,170,171
    description 73
    feeding...........................76
    field recognition 76
    habits 76
    range 76
    reproduction 75
Flights 150,164
    ringing 159,182
    to upland game 159,163
    to waterfowl 163,167,184
    to owls 182
Frounce 149

Game birds 176,177
    upland 180
Game-hawking 184
Gamekeeping 86,87
Gloves 95,106
Grouse 178,188
Goshawks 55-61
    description 53
    field recognition 58,60
    historical use................. 55,60
    range 57,58
    subspecies 58
Golden Eagle 84,170-171
Gyrfalcon........................... 41-45
    breeding 44
    description 41,44
    historical use 44,45
    range 42,44

Haggard Hawk 111
Halsband 148
Harris Hawk 12,47,150,169,170
    description 79
    habits 82
    range 79
    reproduction 79
Hawk, forest 12,50
Hawk, history of......................47
Hawk, marsh 116
Hawk, mountain 87,111
Hawk, rough-legged 139
Hawk, Swainson's 183
Hood(s) 95,100
Hooding................... 102,151,144
Hybrids.............................16

Imping 132
Incubation...........................14
In yarak 173

Jess(es) 95,97

Kestrel 17-19,50
Kite 184

Leash............................ 95,99
Legality 7,47,48,60,61
Leopold, Aldo S. 89
Losses 157
Lure(s) 12,97,108,145,151
Lure bags 110
Lure flying 142-143,152,153
Lure training 108,145

Meadowlark 190-193
Merlin 21,22
Moulting 134,135

Passager(s) 111,123,124,125,126,127,132
Peregrine 13,14,33,161,162
    flight 39
    range 33

subspecies 37
training..........................161
Peregrine, Peale's 39
Perch(es) 104,105
Pole luring 156
Prairie falcon..........................27
   breeding 29
   description 27
   field recognition 28
   habitat 27
   migration 27
   range 27
   training..........................29

Quarry 12,190
   wild quarries 160-162
   release quarries 163
   flock 181

Red-tailed Hawk 169,170
   description 67
   field recognition 69
   habits 69,70
   historical use......................69
   lifespan..........................70
   range 67
   reproduction 71
   subspecies 69

Saker falcons.................... 40-44,90
Set 159,147
Sharp-shinned Hawk...................49
   description 49
   feeding..........................52
   historical use.................... 50,51
   life-span 179
   range 50
   subspecies 50
Sparrowhawk 47,48,50
Swivel(s) 95,98

Thyroid extract 134
Training 13
   advanced 164-167
   early 129-131
Traps....................113-114,115,118

Upland game 144,187

Vermin 13,83

Waiting on............................39
Waterfowl 114,184,185
Wilson's snipe............. 162,190,191,192

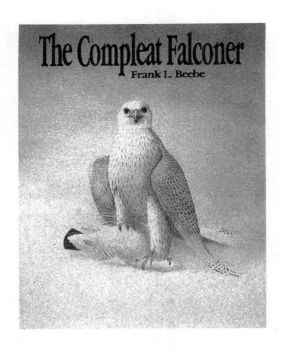

The Compleat Falconer
Frank L. Beebe
ISBN 0-88839-253-2
$8^{1}2$ x 11 336 pp.
Over 250 illustrations and 32 original paintings

Frank L. Beebe—the falconer: for forty years one of North America's leading falconers. His previous books on the subject are largely responsible for the present status and popularity of this ancient sport.

Frank L. Beebe—the researcher: he is not only a leading Peale's and Gyr falcon researcher but also the pioneer falcon breeder.

This major work is totally new in writing, sketches and paintings. It brings together the contemporary summation of what the sport is about, where it has been and where it is going. This treatise will serve the non-initiated admirably and stimulate the experienced. The marvelous color paintings represent the intuitive under-standing of this unusual man.